THE OMISSION OF THE HOLY SPIRIT FROM
REINHOLD NIEBUHR'S THEOLOGY

THE OMISSION OF THE HOLY SPIRIT

From Reinhold Niebuhr's Theology

RACHEL HADLEY KING

PHILOSOPHICAL LIBRARY
New York

To
DOCTOR MARGARET DANN
IN GRATITUDE AND LOVE

TABLE OF CONTENTS

TABLE OF CONTENTS (*Continued*)

FOREWORD

Reinhold Niebuhr's ethics and doctrine of sin require a God who is righteous and therefore other than the universe. His science-conditioned confidence that all events in the created universe have their causes in previous events in the created universe makes it impossible for him to believe in miracle and so rules out a belief in the Holy Spirit, in a genuine Incarnation, and in the continued existence of Jesus Christ after Calvary. But if God permanently discarded Jesus at Calvary God neither respects human personality nor is righteous or loving. This disastrously undermines the doctrine of God's righteousness which is essential to Niebuhr's ethics and doctrine of sin.

This book was begun in Colorado in the summer of 1954 and a large part of it was written in University Park, Denver. As *The Omission of the Holy Spirit From Reinhold Niebuhr's Theology* goes to press, I would like to thank the Mary Reed Library of the University of Denver for its courtesy and assistance to me. But the book was written during many school vacations and in many places, and my thanks are also due to the Yale University and Union Theological Seminary Libraries for their kindness and help. It has been a pleasure to work with Mr. Thomas Kiernan and Mrs. Rose Morse of the Philosophical Library, Publishers, whose skill and consideration have been very helpful. Also I wish especially to express my gratitude to Dr. Luther A. Weigle, Dean Emeritus of the Yale Divinity School, for his steady expression of encouragement and confidence.

RACHEL H. KING

East Northfield, Massachusetts
July, 1963

CHAPTER I

INTRODUCTION: THE PREDICAMENT POSED BY THE ABSENCE OF THE HOLY SPIRIT

THE CONSENSUS of opinion among the interpreters of Reinhold Niebuhr's theology is that the greatest lack in his thinking is the absence of any well worked out doctrine of the Holy Spirit.[1] The implication has been that it is regrettable that a man who has written so voluminously and cogently on many aspects of the Christian faith should have neglected to round out his thinking by including in it a carefully worked through discussion of this important item in Christian belief.

It is the contention of this essay that the omission is not accidental but is essential to the whole structure of Reinhold Niebuhr's thought.

His basic thinking is irreconcilable with the presuppositions that underlie the doctrine of the Holy Spirit. This traditional Christian doctrine presupposes a belief in a loving God who is other than the creation, who, by the intimate intercourse of his Spirit with the lives of men, regenerates, sanctifies, strengthens, and guides them into an increasingly complete companionship with himself. God is other than the creation and men are part of the creation.

---

[1] Gordon Harland, *The Thought of Reinhold Niebuhr.* (New York: Oxford University Press, 1960) p. 150; Paul Lehman, "The Christology of Reinhold Niebuhr" in Charles W. Kegley and Robert W. Bretall, editors, *Reinhold Niebuhr His Religious, Social and Political Thought.* (New York: The Macmillan Company, 1956) pp. 277, 278; Hans Hofmann, *The Theology of Reinhold Niebuhr* (New York: Charles Scribner's Sons, 1956) p. 246.

So God's conscious direct guiding and strengthening of a human life by his Spirit in his personal care for individuals involves sporadic divine action in the world in a way other than the standard routines which his constant action regularly employs in his steady upholding of nature.

But the standard routines of nature, when viewed from within the world, are the stuff with which science deals. And science has impressively documented its claim that the ongoing of nature is by the unbroken sequences of these standard routines. From the point of view of science, therefore, the unpredictable influence of the Holy Spirit upon a human life[1] would be the sporadic breaking of the creation barrier by a power which is beyond nature, that is, by a supernatural God. Even if this influence of the Holy Spirit is thought of as being only upon the spirits of men, nevertheless a man's intellectual-spiritual activity has a concomitant neural activity, and if the man obeys the influence of the Holy Spirit he will upon some occasions rearrange the gross physical matter of the world in a way that he would not otherwise have done. (He might upon a particular occasion carry a basket of food to someone in need instead of knocking a golf ball down a fairway.) From the point of view of a supernatural God this action of the Holy Spirit upon a human spirit would seem to be only an advantageous intensifying of, or modifying the manner of expression of, the power that he constantly exerts with respect to the creation. (Throughout this book I use *supernatural* in the non-spacial sense in which St. Augustine and William Temple describe God's relation to the world.)[2] But from the point of view of science, which is enmeshed in the observance only of nature in its standard routines, this action of the Holy Spirit would seem to involve a breaking of the creation barrier to modify nature by the insertion of supernatural power. *In other words, from the point of view of science,*

---

[1] John 3:7, 8.
[2] See Appendix A.

belief in the traditional Christian doctrine of the activity of the Holy Spirit involves miracle.

That the problem of miracle is still the basic difficulty in relating intellectually scientific and Christian beliefs is the theme of William G. Pollard's book, *Chance and Providence*. Dr. Pollard is both a noted physicist and Executive Director of the Oak Ridge Institute of Nuclear Studies, Tennessee, and an ordained minister of the Episcopal Church, and so is one of the few people with a high degree of professional training in both disciplines. According to Dr. Pollard the problem is that

> It is a most difficult thing for the scientifically trained mind to conceive how God could act in His world. From the standpoint of science every event is the product of empirically ascertainable antecedents with which it is causally related. To speak of an event as an act of God, or to say that it happened because God willed that it should, seems a violation of the whole spirit of science. The scientifically trained man will counter such an assertion with cogent and apparently inescapable arguments. He will assert that the cause of any event is subject to scientific investigation and experimental verification. He will point to numerous examples of phenomena which in past ages were universally regarded as divinely caused but which are now understood quite adequately and even simply in terms of known scientific laws. He will insist that the only proper attitude is one of suspended judgment until the matter can be properly studied. He will further require that every suggested explanation, including the possibility of God's action, be clearly labeled hypothetical until it has been experimentally verified. Since no one can imagine how to produce an experimental verification of the Divine activity, this usually settles the matter.[1]

[1] William G. Pollard, *Chance and Providence* (New York: Charles Scribner's Sons, 1958), p. 7.

3

Dr. Pollard's own theory, that the indeterminism of quantum mechanics offers the structural basis within nature for the possibility of miracle, is an excellent and frank attempt to pinpoint the problem and deal constructively with it Much more work needs to be done along the lines of thought that his book opens up. *Chance and Providence* was published too late for its theory to be available in the forming of Reinhold Niebuhr's theology. Niebuhr's theology therefore has to struggle with the religious difficulties raised by the rise of scientific thought without the partial help afforded by Dr. Pollard's work.

The three characteristic postulates of Reinhold Niebuhr's religious position are his love of the Bible, the Hebraic progression of his thought according to ethical rather than metaphysical logic, and his acceptance of the overall claims made by the sciences in their respective fields. Although the problems raised by science are a major factor in the creation of that theologically monistic Liberalism against which Niebuhr has always reacted so violently, he, like Liberalism, assumes the authority of science. He insists that "religious affirmations" should be brought "into harmony with scientific facts,"[1] and that "the facts, known by natural science . . . (are) indisputable on their own level."[2] "The metaphysical problem of religion cannot be depreciated. In the long run religion must be able to impress the mind of modern man with the essential plausibility and scientific respectability of its fundamental affirmations."[3] He admits the truncating influence of science on theology. "If we take the disciplines of the various sciences seriously, as we do," he says, "we must depart at one important point from the biblical picture of life and history. The accumulated evidence of the natural sciences convinces us that the realm of natural causation is more closed, and less subject to divine intervention, than the

---

[1] DCNR. p. 9e. For the key to references to Niebuhr's works see the bibliography.
[2] FH. p. 167b.
[3] DCNR. p. 16cd.

4

biblical world view assumes."[1] "The pure sciences have revealed a world of nature much more impersonal and, seemingly, much less amenable to a divine will and to human needs than had been traditionally assumed."[2] "Since every natural phenomenon can be explained in terms of a preceding one the myth becomes useless when science discovers the chain of causation."[3] "And the course of nature is more subject to inflexible law than the Bible supposes."[4] "There can be no question but that the development of the physical sciences has permanently increased the difficulty of justifying the personalization of the universe upon which all religious affirmations are based."[5] The "corruption of religion into a bad science has aroused the justified protest of a scientific age."[6] "That part of mythology which is derived from prescientific thought, which does not understand the causal relations in the natural and historical world, must naturally be sacrificed in a scientific age."[7] "Whenever orthodoxy insists upon the literal truth of such myths it makes a bad historical science out of true religious insights."[8] "Religion

---

[1] CRPP. p. 197cd.

[2] DCNR. p. 5de.

[3] T in M. p. 131cd.

[4] CRPP. p. 197f. The quotation continues: "In other words, we have given up one kind of miracle, and miracle is the dearest child of faith. We do not have difficulty with all miracles. The healing miracles of Jesus, for instance, are credible because we recognize the depth and height of spirit in the dimension of each personality and the consequent spiritual dimension of bodily ill. Psychosomatic medicine corroborates such a conception." This is not the vital issue. It is a confusion as to what constitutes a miracle. If created mind has an effect upon created body as psycho-somatic medicine claims, then in spite of the mystery of the freedom of the human spirit and its relation to the bio-chemical reactions of the body the transaction takes place wholly *within* the creation. Thus the crucial question is not raised as to whether a God, wholly supernatural to the creation, can sporadically bring his influence to bear upon it at will in a special way in order to further certain particular results that he wishes to obtain.

[5] DCNR. p. 11bc.

[6] FH. p. 33c.

[7] T in M. pp. 118f, 119a.

[8] T in M. p. 128d. Included among myths according to Niebuhr are: the Creation and the Fall, T in M. p. 128e; the God-man, T in M. p. 129c; the Atonement, (1)HN. p. 94b; the Resurrection, BT. p. 304d.

had no right to insist on the scientific accuracy of its mytho-logical heritage. From this position a retreat was neces-sary."[1]

And yet Niebuhr knows that when simple faith in a supernatural God personally at work in his world is given up part of the transforming and driving power of religion is lost. And so it has come about that "Religious faith in both Catholic and Protestant versions of Christianity and in the Jewish version of Biblical faith survives most vitally in backward 'regions,' that is, in those sections of culture in which the failure of religion to come to terms with the un-doubted truths disclosed by the disciplines of philosophy and the sciences is not found too embarrassing."[2] "Naive religions have frequently been morally more potent than highly rationalized ones."[3] "The religious groups which are still ambitious to defy civilization in the name of their faith have a theology which cannot gain the respect of the thoughtful leaders of modern life."[4]

In spite of what Niebuhr believes to be the truncating effect of science upon Christianity, his basic Hebrew assump-tion that God is righteous forces him to discard all Panthe-istic—and this includes all Idealistic, Naturalistic, "Emer-gent," or otherwise Monistic—attempts to equate God with the universe.[5] This repudiation of Pantheism makes inaccess-ible for Niebuhr a spurious redefined use of the term "Holy Spirit" that can be employed by those who are willing to claim to teach Christianity in pulpit and divinity school at the same time that they are willing to discard the basic Jewish-Christian belief that God is righteous in favor of a belief in some form of philosophical Monism. For if one holds any form of Pantheistic theology, which in some

---

[1] T in M. p. 118f.
[2] SDH. p. 147bc.
[3] DCNR. p. 214e. And see BT. p. 126de.
[4] DCNR. p. 187bc.
[5] DCNR. p. 214a-d; REE. p. 198a-f; T in M. p. 123a-f; DCNR. p. 14b-d;
(1) HN. pp. 22f, 23a; FH. pp. 103e, 137c.

6

way or to some extent equates God with the universe, then the beneficial aspect of nature and the impulses toward moral goodness and love in the human heart can be called the Holy Spirit. But this interpretation of the term is out of the question for Niebuhr because Niebuhr's awareness of human sin keeps him from being a Pantheist. And Niebuhr's acceptance of the restricting effect of science upon religious thought renders inaccessible to him a belief in the traditional Christian doctrine of the function of the Holy Spirit.

For in the Jewish-Christian tradition God is the purposeful, energetic, righteous Creator. Inasmuch as the world contains evil, if God is the Creator of the world and perfectly righteous he must be other than the creation. Therefore the Holy Spirit or the Holy Ghost must also be other than the creation. As we have seen, this means that the activity of the Holy Spirit in regenerating, sanctifying, and strengthening the Christian, and in illuminating scripture for his guidance involves miracle. The progression of Niebuhr's thought is along ethical rather than along philosophical lines. If one recalls his tremendous emphasis on human sin one realizes that he would have to think of God as supernatural or else think of him as being in some way a constituent part of human wickedness. The result is that the combined scientific and moral presuppositions of Niebuhr's thinking leave him with confidence in a supernatural righteous God but with no way of explaining how this God can have personal contact with or be personally available to the lives of men.

For in traditional Christian teaching it is a function of the Holy Ghost to be the method of God's communication with the world at the personal level. In addition, therefore, to the work of the Holy Ghost in assisting the individual believer's growth in the Christian life the Nicene Creed declares that the Holy Ghost "spake by the Prophets," and that when God wished to effect men's salvation the "Lord Jesus Christ . . . was incarnate by the Holy Ghost of the Virgin Mary." But if one denies on principle the supernatural God's ability to communicate at the personal level with his creation, one cannot deny it at one point only but one is forced to deny it all along the line. This would mean that one would be at a loss to explain how God could reveal himself to men in the Old Testament period, or become incarnate in one particular human life.

We shall find that these two difficulties pervade all of Niebuhr's theology. Being unable to think of God as communicating at will with the creation at the personal level he cannot adequately substantiate his claim that Christianity is a God-revealed instead of a man-invented religion. And his thinking reduces the Incarnation to the human Jesus,[1] "a Jewish teacher, rabbi, and prophet who made messianic claims for himself,"[2] whose tragic death[3] becomes the "Christ event,"[4] because in it the relation of God's love to his justice[5] is most clearly seen.[6]

From the point of view of the practical religious life what Niebuhr's Neo-orthodoxy turns out to be is a kind of Prophetic Deism. It does not appear to be a permanently tenable religious position. It breaks down internally on the ethical issue upon which all Niebuhr's thought is based. For he abandons Liberalism on the grounds that it has no place for the fact that man is a sinner because he has given priority to self-love instead of devotion to the righteous-loving God. This means that Niebuhr's thought to be consistent would have to substantiate the traditional Christian claim that God is righteous and loving. For if God is not righteous-loving, disloyalty to him is not the terrible sin that Niebuhr claims it to be and so Niebuhr's brilliant apology for the sinfulness of man is discredited. It is not sinful to be unsubmissive to brute power or to unethical power. As William

---

[1] REE. p. 287a-d; DCNR. p. 80ab.
[2] FH. p. 142cd.
[3] BT. p. 192de; (2) HD. p. 81cd.
[4] SDH. p. 91b.
[5] (2) HD. p. 56e.
[6] T in M. pp. 134e-135b; SDH. pp. 65f, 66a.

Temple says: *"The essential principle of spiritual authority is the evocation by Good of appreciation of itself; for only when this occurs is authority exercised over the spirit."*[1]

But since Niebuhr cannot believe in Jesus Christ as the actual incarnation of deity (but only as the perfect symbol of the divine love), Calvary is proved to be only man's gift of costly devotion to God, not the gift of God's costly devotion to man. Furthermore, since Niebuhr cannot believe in the actual incarnation of Deity, and since he cannot believe that God breaks the creation barrier, he does not believe that Jesus Christ rose from the dead as a person but only as his disciples' human memory of him energized their hearts. And the immortality of the soul Niebuhr denies. His theology therefore has no place in it for any personal expression of gratitude on the part of God to Jesus of Nazareth for the costly devotion of his agonizing death. Niebuhr insists that Calvary symbolizes the suffering love in the heart of God, but actually Niebuhr's God completely ignores Calvary.

But if God really ignored Jesus at Calvary, if "every individual is a Moses who perishes outside the promised land,"[2] if Jesus' agonized cry on the cross, "My God, my God, why hast thou forsaken me?" was only the prelude to the permanent extinction of his personal life, then God is not righteous-loving. And so Jesus' whole ethical teaching had been based upon a mistaken estimate of the character of God. If God allowed Jesus as an individual to die permanently on Good Friday then God has not even the moral decency of the very human masters in Jesus' parables who lavishly reward their faithful servants. *The character and reputation of Almighty God are at stake in the Resurrection.*

For Niebuhr Jesus is not the risen Lord at the right hand of the Father but only the Suffering Servant of the

---

[1] William Temple, *Nature, Man and God* (London: Macmillan, 1951), p. 345.

[2] (2) HD. p. 308c; (2) HD. p. 81cd; FH. pp. 9ab, 63d, 77cd; and see (1) HN. p. 164b.

fifty-third chapter of Isaiah. But even on the original Old Testament terms it is impossible to think of a merely suffering servant of the righteous God. For after the Servant had "poured out his soul to death" and they had "made his grave with the wicked" "he shall divide the spoil with the strong" and "prolong his days," and "see the fruit of the travail of his soul and be satisfied."[1] As the prophet was probably thinking of the Suffering Servant in terms of the Jewish nation he could envisage the nation's reward in re-established prosperity after its vicarious suffering without raising the question of whether the individual has a life after death. But the moment the Suffering Servant is thought to be an individual human being in the person of the Messiah, as Jesus and Reinhold Niebuhr both interpret him to be, then the belief in the life after death becomes a necessary interpretation of the wording of the great prophecy. *It is one thing to claim that when any man, including Jesus, serves God, that it is the duty of that man to love and serve God with such complete devotion that he takes no thought for his personal safety and welfare either in life or death. It is another thing entirely to claim that it does not matter for the character of God whether or not God did cherish the person of Jesus after his death and express gratitude to him for his self-sacrificing service. Ingratitude is not morally neutral. It is a sin. A God who permanently discarded the individual called Jesus of Nazareth at Calvary would be a God who was not morally worthy of the devotion Jesus had given him.*

Of course there is nothing new in the denial of Jesus' Resurrection. The denial has been typical of twentieth century Liberalism. But as Niebuhr points out, Liberalism has tied itself in with Western cultural and philosophical insights rather than with the Bible for its nourishment. Once return to the Bible as Niebuhr does and take seriously its insights about the righteousness of God and the sinfulness of man

---

[1] Isaiah 53:9-12.

and the question of the Resurrection of Jesus cannot be side-stepped.

Although Reinhold Niebuhr's thought has matured in its ethical, social, and political aspects as he has watched the shifting world affairs for the past generation, his interpretation of the relation of science to religion has remained basically constant. His difficulty in believing that a righteous God who is other than the creation can on specifically chosen occasions interact with some portion of his creation at the personal level has continued to limit his thinking in the areas of the activity of the Holy Spirit, Revelation, the Incarnation, and the Resurrection. Since it is with this constellation of ideas that this essay deals it has seemed wise to use the systematic rather than the chronological method in discussing his writings. If one were discussing his political thought, the chronological method would be advisable.[1]

It should be needless to add that religiously Reinhold Niebuhr is greater than the inadequacies of his theological system. The prophetic devotion of his long life of service to a God who, he feels confident, is righteous and loving, even though his intellectual belief does not furnish him with sufficient grounds for believing him to be so, is in itself an impressive Christian witness. Niebuhr's contribution to the Christian life and thought of the twentieth century can scarcely be overestimated. The inadequacies of his thought can be traced to the intellectual straight-jacket into which the claims made in the name of science have cramped his belief. He has steadily refused to come to terms with these claims by surrendering his Christian heritage to a non-Biblical conception of an immanent God. At one stroke Niebuhr cut away all the typical twentieth century prattle about God being the little spark of the divine in each of us and returned to the supernatural Biblical God who is righteous, who demands righteousness from men, and who punishes unrighteousness. In the period between the First and

---

[1] See Appendix C.

11

Second World Wars it was a message many were hungry to
hear. Those of us who were struggling with Liberalism in
the 1930s will never forget the thrill we felt when we first
read *Beyond Tragedy*. It was a rock in a weary land. It
was a message from home.

CHAPTER II

THE PREDICAMENT POSED BY SCIENCE AND ETHICS

HISTORICALLY CHRISTIANITY is a pre-scientific religion trying now to cope with the problems of a scientific age. The realization of this fact conditions the whole of Reinhold Niebuhr's theology. He is aware both that theoretical science challenges basic Biblical assumptions about the nature of existence and that applied science in the twentieth century's technological development has greatly increased the difficulty of the practical application of Christian ethics. The problem admitted of no easy solution for him for he is from first to last the Christian prophet and pastor in his outlook, committed to the spiritual guidance of men and to the Bible as the determiner of the line of direction of Christian belief.

The question of the relation of science to Christianity began to be acute in the seventeenth century, and Lord Herbert of Cherbury's five articles of natural religion laid the groundwork for the English Deism which thought of God as unconnected with the present world as the watchmaker is at present unconnected with the perfect watch which he has previously contrived and set going. Lord Herbert's five articles are: "1. That there is some supreme divinity. 2. That this divinity ought to be worshipped. 3. That virtue joined with piety is the best method of divine worship. 4. That we should return to our right selves from sins. 5. That reward or punishment is bestowed after this life is finished."[1]

---

[1] Harold R. Hutcheson, editor and translator, *Lord Herbert of Cherbury's De Religione Laici. . . . with a Critical Discussion of his Life and Philosophy* (New Haven: Yale University Press, 1944), p. 129.

The Christian inadequacies of this position are obvious and have often been stressed: it has too optimistic a view of unaided human nature's ability to be virtuous; it offers no explanation of why there had to be a revelation to the Old Testament prophets or why Christ had to die for man's salvation, and it has no place for present divine assistance to the struggling Christian, that is, no place for God's grace given to man by means of the regenerating, guiding, and strengthening power of the Holy Spirit. That the Enlightenment could consider Deism adequate while it contained such lacks is an evidence of "the easy conscience of modern man" which Niebuhr thinks has so widely missed the mark of true insight.[1]

But faced as we are in the twentieth century with various brands of Naturalism which are put forward as philosophical substructures for Christianity there are certain Christian advantages to early Deism which it is well not to overlook. The problem that was beginning to face Christian thought in the seventeenth century was the problem of miracle. Traditional Christian interpretation had claimed that Jesus literally stilled the tempest, walked on the water, raised the dead, and multiplied the loaves and fishes. In view of the successful investigation of the regularities of nature such abnormalities in day to day experience seemed impossible.

The public attack on the scientific respectability of belief in miracles by those who claim any interest at all in religion has always been focused on what might be called the physically gross miracle stories of the gospels. Since any one of the above mentioned miracle stories is, *taken by itself,* on the periphery of religious importance, those who privately denied all miracle could express disbelief in these spectacular occurrences on the ground of scientific impossibility without seeming to say, "Christianity in its entirety is a mistake." And hard pressed apologists, who were at the same time genuinely devoted Christians, could try to escape the di-

---

[1] (1) HN. Chapter IV.

lemma caused by science by insisting that "man shall not live by bread alone," and that the "spiritual" side of religion was what was most important and that this was the center of their faith. The fallacy in this "exclusively spiritual" position is that Christianity is something more than an interrelation of values.

What some devoted divinity school professors and most of the devout Christian laity have not clearly seen is that if one denies miracle *in principle*—as distinct from being skeptical as to whether Moses' rod on a particular occasion turned into a snake[1]—one is completely denying the work of grace in the human heart on the part of the Holy Spirit, and the revelation of God to the Old Testament prophets, and the Incarnation and the Resurrection of Christ; and that if one denies all this one has completely repudiated New Testament Christianity. This is why the disbelief in miracle has gradually permeated and undermined Christian theology in its "spiritual" aspects. There has been a hesitancy on the part of Liberal and Neo-orthodox divinity schools to undertake the much needed work of a frank grappling with this central intellectual problem because professors have been so unsure in their own beliefs that they have hesitated to state simply and frankly to the world where they really do stand on this important question. By tacit consent in theological circles this important problem is skillfully by-passed. The by-passing has been greatly assisted by the current fashion of a high degree of departmentalization in theological studies and by the current fashion for "objective" teaching: one can talk endlessly and glowingly of what St. Paul believed without going on record as to whether or not St. Paul's belief was as a matter of fact correct. The by-passing has also been facilitated both by the humility of the callow young divinity students, who ascribe their own intellectual confusion to their scholarly immaturity, and by the confidence of the students in the

---

[1] Exodus 4:2-4.

ability and integrity of the faculty. The obscurantism continues from generation to generation because by the time the student really has a clear picture of what the theological situation really is he is so far along the professional road that he falls into line for professional reasons. And so he accepts the pervasive tacit assumption that one says one thing to the laity and a slightly different thing when one is with one's professional equals, and that in sermons one must simplify and slightly falsify what one actually believes, or speak with an evasiveness that carries one type of meaning to the simple minded and a slightly opposite meaning to the initiated, because one must "talk down" to a congregation so that they will comprehend what one is saying.[1] It is not that an average congregation with a fair sprinkling of college trained members could not understand what the minister was saying. The real truth is that a great many ministers do not dare put what they really believe into words of one syllable, even to themselves. And the students' professors were caught in the same intellectual-professional dilemma when they in turn were students in the previous generation.

When the problem of miracle first became acute three centuries ago, Lord Herbert's five articles appeared to many to restate basic religion with miracle omitted. In spite of the shallowness of his position it deserves more serious and respectful Christian consideration than is usually given it. For among the few basic alternatives to the Christian position it allows for the conservation of the Biblical insistence on the all powerful, intelligent, righteous Creator God. The Creator God is not found in Idealism or Pantheism. And

---

[1] The idea that one needs to "talk down" to a congregation is sheer wishful thinking. I have taught for thirty years at the secondary school level and I know that the basic traditional beliefs of Christianity and the basic beliefs of religious interpretations opposed to Christianity can be made clear in simple language to high school sophomores. And I regularly teach bright high school seniors the *Bhagavad-Gita,* the *Phaedo* of Plato and the *Confessions* of St. Augustine and they enjoy it.

both Idealism and Pantheism eventually undercut the description of God as righteous.

Basic Deism allows for God as the powerful and intelligent creator, the perfect watchmaker who contrived the world and set it going. This is to admit miracle at the beginning of the world, for it is to admit that in the act of creation the earth underwent modification by a power outside itself. If on the fifth day, according to pre-evolutionary thinking,[1] God created out of nothing the sea creatures and birds, their creation would have been a modification of the world-as-created-on-the-first-four-days, and the modification would have been brought about by a power exterior to or other than created nature and so would be technically an instance of miracle. As creation happened only once and a very long time in the past it could be thought of as in no way interfering with the unbroken regularities of nature that seventeenth century science was describing. The intelligibility of the world was happily accounted for on this theory by the intelligence of the Creator. And the fact that God was definitely other than the world and only its absentee landlord made it possible for this theory to think of him as righteous and not part of the world's evil. To that extent Deism is more congenial to Biblical religion than is any of the many varieties of Pantheism. The difficulty with any Pantheistic theory is that it so closely identifies God's existence with that of the world that it is impossible to say that God is perfectly righteous inasmuch as the world contains evil as well as good. On the Deistic view God could be thought of as creating physical nature and as setting it running according to unbreakable rules of his own contrivance, the laws of nature. In spite of the clock work description of the lower creation the assumption was that man was free, and this assumption was buoyed up by all the personal elation attending scientific discoveries, legal and governmental advances, and the exploration and colonization of the Western hemisphere.

---

[1] Genesis 1:20-23.

On the Deistic view man can be thought of as having been endowed by God with a divinely implanted faculty called "natural light." This enables men to recognize the basic Moral Law, which reflects God's intelligent righteousness and which it is man's duty to freely follow. This is implied in Lord Herbert of Cherbury's five articles of faith which include the claims that virtue is God's true service; that man must repent of wrong doing; and that there are rewards and punishments after death. Man on this theory has the requirement and the ability to serve God by living the virtuous life and to fulfill this service to God entirely on his own without any outside help from God in the form of strength or guidance which would involve God's interference with the creation and so would involve miracle. On this theory God does not have to be disinterested in the affairs of the world. To use an anachronistic figure of speech the Deistic God can be thought of as intimately watching the affairs of men by celestial television; and his meting out of rewards and punishments after death can be thought of both as carrying to a successful completion the picture of God as righteous, and as giving evidence of his constant intense interest in the creation experiment. Since on this theory God's rewards come after death his interference only takes place in the realm beyond this present world and so again miracle is pushed beyond the confines of nature in its day to day ongoings which science investigates.

Deism, although inadequate, could be used as a first working hypothesis for the coexistence of Christianity and science, and it has been mentioned here at length both because it keeps the righteous Creator-God of the Bible more adequately than do either of the two prevalent contemporary theories of Idealism and Pantheism (under which broad heading are also grouped all forms of Naturalism in which the Divine somehow emerges or attains full adequacy of Being in the course of the process). Deism is also mentioned at length because Reinhold Niebuhr, as we shall see

18

later, is closer to Deism in some aspects of his thought than he would like to admit.[1]

On the subject of respect for the authority of science Niebuhr is a true child of the Enlightenment. In spite of the fact that the problems raised by science are a major factor in the creation of that theological Liberalism against which Niebuhr has always reacted so violently, he assumes the authority of science and assumes that religion must come to terms with its findings.[2]

With a background of the twentieth century's theological inadequacy the young Niebuhr came to a pastorate in Detroit in 1915 fresh from his Liberal theological training at Yale Divinity School, and began his task of reformulating theology to meet the practical moral problems[3] made acute by the impersonality and the high degree of organization that characterize industrialized Western culture.[4] He found that his Liberal theological training was inadequate[5] to meet the situation and he revolted from Liberalism.[6] Niebuhr inveighed against Liberalism for its shallow and sinful assumption of the essential goodness and the moral self sufficiency of human nature. This was not a world of people happily engaged in sloughing off the remnants of barbarism which were due to the evolutionary lag in civilization.[7] Instead he saw a feverish world in which as industrial and national power increased greater scope was given to the inherent sinful human tendency to grab power at the

---

[1] "The withdrawal of God distinguishes deism from theism, which maintains the 'immanence' or continued activity of God in the universe. To the theist, obviously, revelation and miracles are credible; to the deist they are not." Harold R. Hutcheson, editor and translator, *Lord Herbert of Cherbury's De Religione Laici. . . . with a Critical Discussion of his Life and Philosophy* (New Haven: Yale University Press, 1944), p. 55.

[2] See *ante,* pp. 4-6.

[3] DCNR. p. 15a-e.

[4] David Wesley Soper, *Major Voices in American Theology* (Philadelphia: The Westminster Press, 1953), pp. 42, 43. DCNR. pp. 125d-126d.

[5] LNTC. p. 79a-d.

[6] REE. p. 204a-e; T in M. p. 127a-f.

[7] (1) HN. pp. 210c, 249f-250a.

expense of righteousness in a futile effort to offset the basic insecurity that men inevitably feel by reason of their mortality.[1]

Niebuhr saw the predicament of the West in general and of Protestantism in particular as due to the triumph of the Renaissance over the insights of the Reformation.[2] The Reformation had been a return to Biblical religion with its emphasis upon the duty of man to live subordinate to the will of God and to direct his human life to work for God's glory. It had emphasized man's sinfulness and need of justification by faith and salvation by God because man does not in fact fulfill this duty.[3] But side by side with the Reformation in the West was the Renaissance with its largely pagan roots.[4] The influence of the Renaissance fostered the idea of the autonomous individual[5] whose goal was the conquest of nature and the enhancement of his own personality.[6] And it is the influence of the Renaissance that won out in the West. Niebuhr sees the basic influence of the Renaissance, the stress on self satisfied and self sufficient man,[7] bent on enhancing his own personality which is unsubmitted to God,[8] as a basic fostering of the basic sin of pride.[9] And Liberalism, according to Niebuhr, has made the basic error of forgetting its Reformation heritage and largely capitulating to the spirit of the Renaissance.[10] He thinks that this accounts for its inability to speak authoritatively to the human predicament in our desperate world situation,[11] hagridden by the "will-to-power" which is "both a direct form and an indirect instrument of the pride which

---

[1] (1) HN. pp. 250bc, 67b-e, 185ef, 193bc; DCNR. p. 161b-f.
[2] (2) HD. pp. 182f-183b.
[3] (2) HD. pp. 211c-f, 148-150.
[4] (1) HN. p. 5a-d.
[5] (2) HD. pp. 150e, 151ab.
[6] (1) HN. p. 66a-c; (2) HD. pp. 163f-164a.
[7] (2) HD. p. 150cd.
[8] (1) HN. pp. 18f-19a.
[9] FH. p. 121bc; (1) HN. p. 170b. And see quotation on p. 140 from CPP.
[10] (1) HN. p. 5d-f; (2) HD. p. 157ab.
[11] (2) HD. pp. 239e-240b, 287c-288a.

Christianity regards as sin in its quintessential form."[1] When Liberalism turned men's attentions toward Jesus, too often it was to urge them to love everybody as Jesus did, with the implication that if we just dealt lovingly with others, others in turn would deal lovingly with us and then everybody would be happy and the kingdom of God would be on earth.[2] Why the perfect love of Jesus should have led him to the Cross was not considered,[3] nor the relation of his death to God's relationship to man.[4] Good and evil were thought of in terms of direct personal relationships and the extent to which human sin can build itself into institutions and carry on a monstrous, more than individual, power over man was likewise overlooked.[5] All this Niebuhr deals with in his brilliant analysis of human sin.

It is only fair to say, however, that the impotence of Liberalism against which Niebuhr reacted was due in part to two more spiritually creditable factors than those he stresses. Those two factors are its loss of belief in a supernatural righteous Creator God due to its capitulation to scientific theory, and its loss of a belief in hell due to its preoccupation with righteousness. These two factors need to be discussed.

As advancing discoveries in physics and chemistry began to make obvious the complicated nature of the material universe, and as advances in astronomy, geology, and biology began to give man some notion of the universe's age and of the slow development of life on this planet, the idea of a righteous "watchmaker" God who made the world and set it going in six days was seen to be obviously inadequate. God's power came to be seen at work in all time and in all

---

[1] (1) HN. p. 192f.
[2] FH. p. 176ef; (2) HD. p. 45e.
[3] (2) HD. pp. 45de, 53cd.
[4] LNTC. p. 85a-e.
[5] MMIS. pp. xia-xiif, xxbc.

places in nature. What we call the laws of nature seemed to turn out to be simply routine workings of divine power. If the Divine Power comes to be thought of as an aspect of Nature itself and not as the activity of a God who is other than nature and who yet controls nature, the subtle shift has been made from Christian Theism to some form of philosophical Monism.

The philosophies by which this Monism is expressed have usually been Idealism or Naturalism. Idealism by reducing existence to the Absolute and its ideas,[1] and Naturalism by describing God as a force within[2] or aspect of Nature[3] are both Pantheistic. Pantheism so successfully equates God with Nature that it denies his uncompromising righteousness, and hence where Pantheism is dominant it cuts the tap root of Jewish-Christian belief,[4] the confidence in the existence of the righteous Creator God. Pantheism is Christianity's most serious rival.

An example of thoughtful scientifically conditioned Idealism is found in Erwin Schrödinger's *Mind and Matter*. He says that

> ... the reason why our sentient, percipient and thinking ego is met nowhere within our scientific world picture can easily be indicated in seven words: because it is itself that world picture. [In dealing with the perplexing question of why many conscious egos concoct one world from their mental experiences he decides that the multiplicity of minds or consciousnesses] is only apparent, in truth there is only one mind. This is the doctrine of the Upanishads. . . . I do believe that this is precisely the point where our present way of thinking does need to be amended, perhaps by a bit of blood-transfusion from Eastern thought.[5]

The problem here is that if we reduce all existence to God

---

[1] (1) HN. p. 23a; T in M. p. 132bc.

[2] T in M. pp. 132ef, 133a.

[3] (1) HN. p. 23a.

[4] T in M. p. 122b-f.

[5] Erwin Schrödinger, *Mind and Matter* (Cambridge: At the University Press, 1958), pp. 52a, 53ae, 55a.

as in the *Bhagavad-Gita* we make God equally hospitable to righteousness and unrighteousness and so in the final analysis indifferent to both. We can think pleasantly enough of the mind of the late Mahatma Gandhi as an aspect of the mind of God. But we cannot think of the mind of the late Adolph Hitler as an aspect of the mind of God without discarding the whole Biblical claim that God is righteous.

The forms of Naturalism are legion, but they differ from Idealism in laying stress upon physical nature, and then making mind an aspect of or derivative from physical nature. Usually Naturalism makes heavy positive use of the theory of Evolution taken in conjunction with the historical development of civilization to stress the claim that nature is of itself value producing and value conserving.[1] It is erroneously assumed that this is sufficient philosophical foundation for our Western assumption that respect for human personality is grounded in the nature of Existence: through our moral struggles and high motives the divine comes to fuller existence. This theory breaks down from the Christian point of view because it deifies nature, and sub-human nature can be shown to be indifferent to righteousness and unrighteousness and to the value of the individual. This can be seen best by applying the theory to imaginary incidents:

Suppose two men were on a raft in the mid-Pacific without radio communication with anyone and one man fell overboard into shark infested waters and the other jumped overboard to try to save him and both were eaten by sharks. Or take a second incident that is a variation of the first incident. Suppose two men were on a raft in mid-Pacific without radio communication with anyone. One man felt that he would have a better chance of survival if he had all the limited food and water for himself, and so to obtain these he fed his comrade to the sharks. Twenty-four hours later a storm swamped the raft and the murderer also was eaten by sharks.

---

[1] T in M. pp. 132ef, 133a.

According to straight Hindu Pantheism these two incidents receive the same basic religious interpretation. The men, the ocean, the sharks, and the raft are manifestations of the one Absolute Being, temporary configurations on the surface of Absolute Being as ripples are temporary configurations on the deep waters of a lake. The untroubled depths of Being are all inclusive and so exhibit exclusiveness to neither "good" nor "evil." It is only the untroubled depths of Being that matter. The man who gave his life to try to prolong his friend's life labored under the delusion that that life as a *particular* good was valuable, and did not see that its temporary existence is simply a fleeting aspect of the all embracing Whole. Likewise the man who murdered his friend to try to prolong his own life labored under the delusion that his own life was a *particular* good and that a particular good could be obtained for his particular self, instead of seeing that his own temporary existence was simply a fleeting aspect of the all embracing Whole. This Hindu philosophy is a religion of salvation that has looked at the full grimness of despair, and offers to obtain for man the longed for peace of at-home-ness in the universe at the price of relinquishing all craving for good or evil, for purpose in the universe, or for the value of the individual. The Absolute has no goal to reach, no virtues to foster. It cannot be said to love, for if love characterized It, It would have an exclusive attitude toward lovelessness, and hence would be a being outside the finite world who could actively side with the loving heroism of the one man and against the selfish treachery of the other. And in siding *for* loving heroism and *against* treacherous selfishness It would have to act for loving heroism in the human sphere, and against treacherous selfishness in the human sphere, and so as an exclusive spirit—not the Whole Show of Existence—It would have to interact in some way with the natural order, and hence not be Pantheistic, but instead be something more nearly approaching the Jewish-Christian conception of God.

The Western variations upon the Pantheistic theme that are being tentatively thrust forward as philosophical under-girdings of the Christian faith have lacked the grimness and the disillusionment of the Hindu Pantheism chiefly because they are less rigorously consistent, and have about them temporarily the remnants of the joyous mood that only confidence in a righteous loving supernatural Creator God can sustain.

These modern Pantheisms stress the spiritual vitality that the upward evolutionary advance in nature evidences. Nature is thought of as creating and conserving value. The spiritual element in nature comes to its fullest expression in man's struggle for goodness. In this the Divine in nature around us makes us feel at home and upholds us as we work in devotion to what is right. Jesus is fitted into the picture as the one most in harmony with the Divine Order of Nature whose spirit still lives in our memory of and devotion to him. As we strive to follow his example we help to build the Kingdom of God on earth.

Not of course that this outline of thoroughgoing Liberal-ism's basic position was often baldly stated in the pulpit. Baldly stated its divergence from Biblical Christianity is so obvious that opposition from the laity would have been aroused. Many ministers have been pushed to a vagueness of wording in their sermons. This has allowed their occa-sional references to one item or another in the total tradi-tional scheme, clothed in a reshuffling of the traditional vocabulary of the Church, to have read into them by the members of the congregation more of the Orthodox doc-trine than as a matter of fact the clergyman actually sub-scribed to. Thus God's delaying action against modern Protestantism's dissipation of Christianity's doctrinal heri-tage has in part worked through what might be called, for want of a better name, the rear-guard valor of the grand-mothers. A book on their contribution to the ongoing belief of the Church would be interesting and surprising, but it probably cannot be documented until the Final Audit.

Niebuhr is correct in claiming that the Neo-pantheistic belief of Liberalism, with its correlative emphasis upon man's spiritual self-help and basic goodness, could only have seemed adequate as long as it did because man had an unduly easy conscience due to the somewhat wilful ignorance of the evil in his own nature.[1] This wilful ignorance was combined with the feeling of self sufficiency caused by an unusually favorable background in the world situation in the half century before 1914.

But it was not merely the sin of human self-deification that fostered the Neo-pantheistic theology of Liberalism. To some degree that philosophy had been gradually forced upon reluctant Christian thinkers as they had tried to adjust theology to science. As we have seen Deism had first attempted to save the righteous supernatural God for theology by pushing the miracle of his interaction with nature to the two extremes of the creation and the life to come, thus clearing the ongoing life on this earth for the unbroken reign of natural law. As further scientific discoveries made a "watchmaker" God seem very unlikely the shift was gradually made to a thought of God as a Divine Aspect or Concomitant to all natural activity. The word Holy Spirit could still be used in the pulpit with the private interpretation that it is the little spark of the Divine within us because God is everywhere present as a part of all things.

But Liberal belief gained scientific respectability at the cost of sacrificing the old confidence in the righteousness of God. For as evil exists within nature in the form of natural occurrences inimical to man's welfare, and in the form of the wickedness of man who is part of nature on this theory, a God who is part of nature must be involved in its evil. If he were not other than nature, that is, not supernatural to nature, he could not be thought of as standing apart from his creation to disapprove the evil aspects of it and to work

---

[1] (1) HN. pp. 204a-205c.

against them. One defines God as the Total at the cost of describing him as morally indiscriminate.[1]

This can be seen clearly enough if we stop talking about generalizations and try to describe Pantheistically the relation of God to the two situations of men adrift on rafts in the mid-Pacific. In each anecdote there are men, sharks, sea, and a raft, all of which are aspects of the Absolute's activity. One story from the human point of view involves sacrificial love and the other from the human point of view involves base treachery. The completion of the stories, however, is the same. The "divine" ending of both stories consists of several sharks in a state of post-prandial contentment. The goodness of the good man is not preserved for future generations by the ongoing order of nature when he himself perishes. For the carry-over of the incident to future generations would occur only as the original sharks came in turn to contribute to the nourishment of other sea creatures. The carry-over of the elements of either raft incident into the future includes only those elements that are completely sub-ethical and sub-spiritual. Nature in both cases carries on to perpetuate its own existence, but does it with complete indifference to the value of human personality as personality and with complete lack of discrimination between the self-sacrificing virtue of one man and the dastardly treachery of the other. According to the Naturalistic philosophy if values are to be preserved and cherished they are preserved and cherished only from generation to generation in human society. If physical nature blocks that transmission, or if it is thwarted by bad human beings, the man of good-will cannot look for outside help from physical nature or from God, for in Pantheism God's activities are the activities of nature and of man who is a part of nature. There are no supernatural activities on God's part that he can bring specifically to bear upon specific human situations in order to help men to be good or to succor men in desperate situa-

---

[1] T in M. pp. 123a-f, 124ef.

tions by taking them to heaven. In Naturalism God is not supernatural.

One meets with the same type of difficulty in the brilliant scientific philosophy of Alfred North Whitehead. The religious aspect of his thought is sub-Christian:

> 'Religion,' declares Whitehead, 'is the vision of something which stands beyond, behind, and within the passing flux of immediate things; something which is real, and yet waiting to be realized; something which is a remote possibility, and yet the greatest of present facts; something that gives meaning to all that passes, and yet *eludes apprehension;* something whose possession is the final good, and yet is *beyond all reach;* something which is the ultimate ideal, *and the hopeless quest.*'[1]

Whitehead also says:

> The presentation of God under the aspect of power awakens every modern instinct of critical reaction. This is fatal; for religion collapses unless its main positions command immediacy of assent.[2]
>
> Science is concerned with the general conditions which are observed to regulate physical phenomena; whereas religion is wholly wrapped up in the contemplation of moral and aesthetic values.[3]
>
> The power of God is the worship He inspires.[4]

These statements of Whitehead's are irreconcilable with Christianity on five accounts. In the first place he thinks of religion as beyond all human reach and as something which

---

[1] Alfred North Whitehead, *Science and the Modern World* (New York: The Macmillan Company, 1929), p. 275. Italics mine. This paragraph is quoted by Reinhold Niebuhr in CPP. p. 201 with the comment, "These paradoxes are in the spirit of great religion."

[2] *Ibid.*, p. 274.

[3] *Ibid.*, p. 265.

[4] *Ibid.*, p. 276.

eludes human apprehension. Christianity, on the contrary, thinks of God as taking the initiative and claims that God is constantly, actively, and purposefully engaged in the attempted prehension of men. Therefore in the second place, the end for Christianity is not the "hopeless quest" but joyous fulfillment. In the third place Whitehead's statement ignores and contradicts the entire Biblical account which throughout describes God as "almighty" and never loses the balance of its parallel emphases upon the complete power and the complete righteousness of Deity. The whole "development" of Hebrew thought revolves around the uneasy attempt to reconcile both emphases at once with practical human experience. In the fourth place the idea of religion being concerned with the "contemplation" of moral values is not in accord with Christianity. The Hebraic-Christian tradition insists that God personally demands *active obedience* to moral values as the test and expression of loyalty to himself. In the fifth place Christianity holds that it is God as both righteous and powerful who inspires worship. This is basically at variance with Whitehead's implication that God's association with moral value is powerless until men, having contemplated moral values, give God power by trying to embody the moral values in concrete situations. There seems in Whitehead's philosophy, as in simple Pantheistic or Naturalistic forms of religion, no way of conceiving God as at once sufficiently powerful and sufficiently detached from the ongoing continuum to bring any non-routine aid to men in particular circumstances.

The same basic problem we have been analyzing occurs if Idealism is followed as a philosophy, for there the universe and all it contains including men are described as ideas in the mind of God. This explains the correspondence of our minds with the world of nature and it explains our ability to communicate with other human minds.[1] What we think of as the human race and the rest of the whole

---

[1] See *ante* p. 22 on Schrödinger.

created universe are interrelated because they are all part of the same thought process of the Absolute Thinker. This makes the treachery of the man in the one incident and the loving heroism of the man in the other incident both part of the thought process of the same God. Again, this theory like the other theories is inadequately equipped to describe God as disliking unrighteousness and as actively discriminating against it.

Niebuhr points out at length that Liberalism is off the track and weakened because under the influence of the Renaissance it has been taking for granted the unspoiled goodness of man. I have tried to point out that Liberalism is also weakened because it has given up a supernatural conception of God in its attempts to adjust itself to science. And without a theory describing God as supernatural there is no theoretical undergirding for Christianity's claim that God is dependably righteous.

Niebuhr is right in putting this main emphasis upon the sin of man in using the freedom afforded by the Renaissance and by Western expansion for autonomous self assertion instead of service to God. He is also right in insisting that Liberalism's shallow confidence in the unspoiled goodness and perfectability of man as well as its tendency to make religion man-centered have fostered this sin.

But in stressing this culpable shortcoming in Liberalism he has not done justice to the holy perplexities with which Liberalism has struggled. This struggle has itself been a loyalty to God on the part of at least an appreciable minority of the exponents of Liberalism, for it has been a genuine loyalty to truth and goodness and all such devotion God accepts as service to himself. Even inadequate or mistaken hypotheses can be of service to him as stepping stones to fuller revelation, when they are honestly put forward in devotion to righteousness, because all devotion to the highest righteousness that one knows is devotion to the righteous God.

One suspects that when the Almighty selected his chosen nation he knew what he was about, and found their tough argumentativeness positively useful in his plan of revelation. That amazing people not only argued with him, they were so devoted to him and so confident in the basic righteousness of their God that they did not hesitate to remonstrate to his face on occasions when he seemed to them to be unrighteous. Thus Abraham said to God concerning Sodom, "Far be it from thee to do such a thing, to slay the righteous with the wicked. . . . Shall not the Judge of all the earth do right?"[1] And Moses says to God after the golden calf incident, "Turn from thy fierce wrath, and repent of this evil against thy people. Remember Abraham, Isaac, and Israel, thy servants, to whom thou didst swear by thine own self, and didst say to them, 'I will multiply your descendants as the stars of heaven.' "[2] So also "David was angry because the Lord had broken forth upon Uzzah," who had touched the ark and fallen dead.[3] And later "David spoke to the Lord when he saw the angel who was smiting the people, and said, 'Lo, I have sinned, and I have done wickedly; but these sheep, what have they done?' "[4] Job is notorious for his willingness to question God: "I would speak to the Almighty, and I desire to argue my case with God. . . . Behold, he will slay me; I have no hope; yet I will defend my ways to his face. This will be my salvation, that a godless man shall not come before him."[5] And Jeremiah is even more daring than Job: "Righteous art thou, O Lord . . . yet would I plead my case before thee. Why does the way of the wicked prosper?"[6] And again, "Wilt thou be to me

---

[1] Genesis 18:25.
[2] Exodus 32:12-13.
[3] II Samuel 6:8.
[4] II Samuel 24:17.
[5] Job 13:3, 15, 16.
[6] Jeremiah 12:1.

31

like a deceitful brook, like waters that fail?"[1] There is no hint that God disapproved of the questioning of these men, or did not deeply respect them. It was through the depth of their trust in his righteousness that they were able to question his seeming unrighteousness and this helped make it possible for God to reveal his righteousness to Israel as to no other nation. And Jesus put the stamp of his approval upon the idea that loyalty to the morally best that one knows is never disloyalty to God by stating that truth conversely when he said, "Whoever says a word against the Son of man will be forgiven; but whoever speaks against the Holy Spirit will not be forgiven, either in this age or in the age to come."[2] Conceivably one might honestly err in one's estimate of Jesus, but speaking against the Holy Spirit is conscious slandering of the Divine at the point where the Divine by its goodness is recognized within the person's own heart as divine.

Unswerving loyalty to truth and goodness is part of the prophetic tradition to which Niebuhr is trying to return. That Liberalism surrendered too much too soon does not mean that some of its ablest exponents, when faced with the developments of modern science, have not sincerely found themselves unable to believe in a supernatural righteous God.[3] Niebuhr himself only escaped this quandary by a confidence in the validity of righteousness as offering true insight into the nature of reality, which enabled him to be willing to try to follow the logic of ethics even if he was forced to leave philosophical consistency at somewhat loose ends.[4]

There was also a moral difficulty within the claims of Orthodoxy itself which had helped weaken its claims in the estimation of Liberal thinkers. The Orthodox doctrine of hell involves the claim that God inflicts upon each of the damned an amount of pain over a million times greater than

---

1 Jeremiah 15:18.
2 Matthew 12:32.
3 DCNR. p. 204a-e.
4 DCNR. p. 214cd; CRPP. p. 203cd; T in M, p. 121bef.

the total of all the pain suffered by all the people on earth during World War II. The ordinary decent citizen's reaction to such an idea is that if God is such a fiend he does not deserve human loyalty.

Theology's attempt to save face for God has never been fully successful. For it can be argued that since heaven and hell are correlative beliefs, if heaven must always be thought of as the free gift of God which even the full surrender of a martyr's death cannot earn as a legal right, there is always the corresponding implication that to some extent eternal hell is also the free gift of God which no human being could sin sufficiently to earn.

Theology's claim that God does not punish a man in hell for his past sins but only for continuing to rebel freely against God is an explanation that just does not ring true psychologically. For evil is a parasite and not on an equal footing with God. Traditional Christianity does not think of God and the devil as two independent equal powers as in the religion of Zoroaster, but thinks of the devil as a fallen angel. Moral evil turns out to be the pursuit in the wrong way of something thought to be desirable. But a man in everlasting intense torture in hell would so obviously have nothing of value to obtain by continuing to rebel that only a madman, if still in possession of freedom of choice, would refuse to surrender. To torture the insane seems to the sensitive conscience of modern times highly unethical. Furthermore, eternal torture is something no human being in his own strength could stand. He would disintegrate under it. For a man to suffer the tortures of hell eternally he would have to be receiving constant strength from God in order to continue to experience the pain. This would put God in the class with those sadistic barbarians who, instead of killing men by torture, torture them up to the limit of endurance and then carefully nurse them back to health so that they can repeat the process.

One of the things desperately needed by modern theol-

33

ogy is a careful reworking of the doctrine of hell.[1] If God is to be considered as positively righteous a description must be given of the stern "no" he permanently says to evil and sin. Heaven and hell are correlative doctrines both having to do with the righteousness of God. If God cannot be thought of as saying "no" to evil and sin our grounds for thinking that he cherishes goodness are undercut. And modern theology's tacit repudiation of the doctrine of hell has contributed to the twentieth century's widespread doubt as to the existence of heaven. Without a strong confidence in a God who successfully backs righteousness men are at loose ends and drift into the practical strategy of, "Let us eat and drink and buy expensive gadgets: there are no pockets in shrouds."

One of the great needs in theology is for a reformulating of the doctrine of hell in a way that will really undergird the belief in the righteousness of God. No full discussion of the righteousness of God and the toughness of the "no" he says to sin is complete without an explicit dealing with his treatment after death of those who persistently desire to oppose his righteousness. If a sensitive conscience increases one's ability to suffer in this life as well as impedes one's practical chances in the mad scramble to get ahead, the young, who as yet have very little knowledge of God, are sure to ask, "Why should I try to be *very* good if I can be more successful and comfortable by following the lower standard accepted as the decent behavior of the ordinary good citizen by society at large, and combining loyalty to a fairly high form of the current social code with a little discreet and law-abiding selfishness? What does the man who suffers to be very good stand to gain by it if the same hydrogen bomb will shortly annihilate both of us as well as the milieu in which we have labored?" It is a question the young have a right to ask and it cannot be adequately answered

---

[1] William Temple makes a strong plea for the necessity of rethinking this doctrine in his *Nature, Man and God* (London: Macmillan, 1951), pp. 455, 456.

without taking into account God's continuing dealings with men after they have died. It is an inadequacy in Niebuhr's ethical thought that he is unable to think in terms of God's dealing with men in a life after death.[1] He lacks the full follow-through to his claim that God is righteous. This omission is in line with his basic belief that the creation barrier cannot be broken. As Incarnation would break the creation barrier from one direction so the traditional Christian belief in life after death would break it from the opposite direction by taking the individual out of our universe.

If Niebuhr completely omits a discussion of hell he has been justly famous for his restatement of the doctrine of original sin. He has made a broadside attack upon Liberalism's easy assumption of man's natural goodness and moral perfectability. Original sin for Niebuhr is not an inherited taint, but is man's inevitable although unnecessitated giving of top priority to his own security when it is threatened by his mortality. It is man's tendency to consider first his own personal welfare:

> Anxiety is the internal description of the state of temptation. It must not be identified with sin because there is always the ideal possibility that faith would purge anxiety of the tendency toward sinful self-assertion. The ideal possibility is that faith in the ultimate security of God's love would overcome all immediate insecurities of nature and history. That is why Christian orthodoxy has consistently defined unbelief as the root of sin, or as the sin which precedes pride. It is significant that Jesus justifies his injunction, 'Be not anxious' with the observation, 'For your heavenly Father knoweth that ye have need of these things.' The freedom from anxiety which he enjoins is a possi-

---

[1] (2) HD. pp. 45ef, 308c; (1) HN. p. 25bc; BT. p. 224cd; DST. p. 99c-f.

35

bility only if perfect trust in divine security has been achieved.[1]

But since, as we shall see later, according to Niebuhr's theory God left the Jesus of history personally in the lurch on Good Friday and did not overcome death on his behalf, man has every right to be anxious in the situation in which he finds himself in this very dangerous world; because Jesus was wrong in thinking that God is the loving heavenly Father who is *actively* concerned with the welfare of individuals. Since the overcoming of death on Jesus' behalf would have involved miracle, Niebuhr, by outlawing miracle from his belief, has undercut his claim that God is dependably loving. This means that he has also somewhat invalidated his claim that man *ought* to trust God rather than his own efforts to gain security. And that in turn somewhat invalidates his claim that it is sinful not to trust in God.

Reinhold Niebuhr tries to simplify the problem of original sin ethically by saying that original sin is not something that we inherited from Adam,[2] that the Garden of Eden story is simply a symbol of the fall that takes place in each person's life when he is old enough to choose and chooses to love himself more than God. For Niebuhr the root sin is self-centeredness. As all men are self-centered all men are on Niebuhr's view sinners.[3] But Professor Niebuhr's modification still does not eliminate the ethical problem as to the character of God, because God created infancy and infancy of itself helps condition a man in the direction of self-centeredness. So apparently by creating infancy God himself to some extent stacks the cards against men.

Through psychology we are learning more and more of the importance of a person's very early life for his later development. Experiences of a child before his second birthday, such as bad frights, can go down into the subconscious

---

[1] (1) HN. pp. 182, 183.
[2] (1) HN. pp. 267e-268a, 269bc.
[3] FH. pp. 121bcef, 122acf.

and cause trouble in his later years. In point of sequence we experience sensation before we experience rational thought. When you pinch an infant's toe it hurts him. When you take his bottle of milk away from him he is hungry. Both are unpleasant situations which he knows immediately from direct sensation and which he does his best to avoid. But when he pulls the cat's tail he does not feel pain and when he overturns the cat's saucer of milk he does not feel hunger, and so he is not immediately aware by direct sensation that these are unpleasant situations. Only several years later will he be mature enough to deduce the cat's unpleasant situation by reasoning that: "What is in the cat's saucer of milk is the same as what is in my mug. If I do not have my milk I am hungry, so if the cat does not have her milk *she* will be hungry. I must not tip over her saucer or the milk will spill and she will be hungry." This hard, complicated thought is beyond the powers of a child barely two years old. The child is simply unable to think responsible thoughts such as these as early as he can feel it to be a misfortune to have his own bottle taken away or his own toe pinched. Of course even at the age of two the child can begin to think and to have some sense of responsibility toward the cat. But even if a sweet tempered fondness for the animal comes naturally to the child, his right treatment of his pet will involve a learned intelligent reaction, not a completely spontaneous one. The baby, however, acts spontaneously for his own advantage long before he can possibly know that there is a God watching over him or that there is a moral righteousness which he is responsible for following. And this situation is entirely of God's creating. I am speaking now of the time before a child is twenty months old. After the child is two years old a rudimentary sense of moral obligation develops and between the ages of two and a half and three and a half the child can begin to be taught about God. I am not saying that a pre-school age youngster cannot be morally responsible in some matters and cannot therefore be a sinner if he does what he knows is wrong. I am only saying that there is an age before which this can be said of him and that age I would put roughly at twenty months. But important learning takes place within this earliest period and it is a period that is self-centered of necessity because of the limitation of the infant's knowledge. When the child at two and a half or three begins to feel a responsibility for someone outside himself he is working against habits already ingrained by the God-devised self-centeredness of infancy.

In Dr. Niebuhr's idea the original fall occurs in each human life when a situation arises in which the individual has to choose between self-centeredness on the one hand and obeying God and the welfare of his neighbor on the other. But it is evident that each individual comes to the all important choice with the cards somewhat stacked against him by the habits acquired in infancy, when he had to direct his action largely on the evidence afforded by sensation and not by rational thought's evaluation of that primary experience. While the self-centeredness acquired in infancy is not itself the will to power that Niebuhr scores so heavily, it is nevertheless a necessary ingredient to it.[1]

And the claim cannot be made that infancy is a result of the Fall. Whether one is thinking in Orthodox, Neo-orthodox, or Liberal terms the first chapter of Genesis in which God tells the birds and sea animals and the human race to be fruitful and multiply, and then saw that all that he had made was good, makes this point especially clear.[2]

---

[1] (1) HN. p. 192cf.
[2] Genesis 1:20-22,26-28,31.

CHAPTER III

BACK TO AMOS

IN HIS EARLY YEARS as a pastor in Detroit Niebuhr became acutely aware of the problems raised by our highly developed organization and technology of big business. Even under the best conditions, when the workers had jobs, the assembly line technique made each worker just a cog in the manufacturing process, thus taking away the craftsman's dignity as the creator of the total finished product. Furthermore, the size of big industries had become so enormous that the people in actual control could not know their employees personally and so keep their individual needs in mind even if they were so inclined. At worst the manufacturing system caused great hardship to the workers when they were laid off in slack periods. The whole system had the tendency to reduce men from their dignified status as individuals to man in the mass, and to make men feel that their individuality as well as their economic security was threatened.[1] It was a situation fraught with social evil. And yet to have seen the leaders of industry simply as ogres would have been to do them an injustice.[2] Responsible though they were they were to a large extent themselves caught[3] within the economic system they were dominating.[4]

The Liberal theology in which Niebuhr had been trained

---

[1] LNTC. pp. 79ab, 80d-f, 154b-f, 155a-c.

[2] (1)HN. p. 225ef.

[3] MMIS. p. 18c-f.

[4] Hans Hofmann, *The Theology of Reinhold Niebuhr* (New York: Charles Scribner's Sons, 1956), pp. 8c-9b, 36-37.

39

offered him no pastoral help in this situation,[1] for behind its exhortations to be good and behind its emphasis on the importance of the individual it had no firm doctrine of the righteousness of God guaranteeing either the ultimate victory of the right or the ultimate welfare of those who served him. Even had Niebuhr been of a docile nature he would not have been able honestly to use religion as an opiate and console the distressed factory workers with the belief that God was watching over them individually and that he would bring them individually to eternal joyous fellowship with himself in the life to come. The misuse of religion as the opiate of the people, while it keeps them socially down trodden, does give them a certain consciousness of human dignity in the thought that they are everlastingly precious to God. But Liberalism, with its taking on of a science-oriented philosophy was not confident that there is a life after death in which God cherishes the individual. The belittling of the hope of heaven by describing it as "By and by, there'll be pie, in the sky" is a gross caricature of the Christian belief in everlasting life, which is sometimes resorted to by those who want to seem spiritually dignified when they deny a basic tenet of Christianity.[2]

On the basis of Liberalism Niebuhr could not have fulminated against the leaders of big business and warned them with evangelistic zeal that they would go to hell unless they bettered the total situation of their employees, for Liberalism had totally given up a belief in hell. One was left in doubt as to whether there was any Power beyond man that really backed the moral law, or whether all its moral exhortations, to caricature them, only amounted to: "Let us all be nice; if everyone were nice, it would be very nice." Many years ago one of my pupils expressed the basic problem when she said to me in class, "What I want to know is, are the commands of Jesus the way it would be nice to run the

---

[1] FH. pp. 31f-32c, 69d, 70cd.
[2] DCNR. p. 181cd.

world if we could, or are they the way God runs the universe?"

Liberalism had also no theology to implement a demand that the industrial system needed overhauling in the interests of righteousness. This is in spite of the fact that Liberalism had specific gains to its credit in ameliorating specific evils within the social system. It had not, however, a theology on which it could challenge basic assumptions of the industrial system. For Liberalism, gradually relinquishing its confidence in the heavenly Creator Almighty before the increasing claims of science, had come to define God in more nearly immanent terms as that power within the universe whose upward thrust into ever better things is evidenced at the biological level by evolution and at the social level by the increasing development and betterment of civilization. Human nature was thought of as essentially good and the momentum of the process itself was thought to guarantee an escalator ride to the world of Utopia. On this interpretation of life there was no religious vantage point from which to criticize that aspect of the process that was manifesting itself detrimentally in the industrial system of the twentieth century, because the Divine was thought of as an integral part of Nature, which idea carried with it the Pantheistic dilemma of neutralizing the character of God with respect to good and evil.

There was an added problem. Communism denied Christianity and in practice ignored the rights of the individual in favor of what it considered the eventual welfare of mass man, which would be the triumph of Communism which would guarantee the safety and happiness of the masses. For all practical purposes this meant that when the Communist party was in control it denied all responsibility to the demands of a righteous God and claimed that any action of lying, treachery, and even of suppressing freedom among the Russian people themselves and causing them great suffering was appropriate action if it furthered the immediate ends of the Communist party.

The Communists had a somewhat more realistic picture of evil than had Liberalism, and this gave them an attractiveness to the disillusioned sufferers within the industrial system. Liberalism had seen evil as the remnant of our animal heritage in the evolutionary process which developing society was progressively sloughing off. This is not a very convincing picture of evil to those who are suffering the ill effects of any rampant injustice. The Communist theory was more realistic. It, too, had confidence in the upward thrust of society but thought that the upward thrust had been interfered with by Capitalism which put the means of production in the hands of a few and so resulted in the oppression of the workers. The inevitable upthrust of history would make the misery of the oppressed a means of uniting them. They would revolt and liquidate Capitalism and institute a classless society of the masses in which each would give according to his ability and take according to his need. Until that time had fully arrived the Communist party was assuming dictatorial control in order to work for this great end.

This was the situation young Niebuhr faced. Basically a religious man and a lover of the Bible, when he came to the parting of the ways he preferred to put his ultimate religious trust in righteousness rather than in metaphysical speculation.[1] To him, as to many other devout persons, the Bible spoke. Reinhold Niebuhr rediscovered and reinstated the prophetic message as it had been proclaimed by Amos. It is one of the most valuable of his many contributions to twentieth century thought. Niebuhr thought of himself as returning to Prophetic thought in general, not to Amos in particular. I am using Amos as an illustration of Prophetic thought because in Amos the view Niebuhr championed is most neatly summarized.[2]

There is a dialectic in history, says Niebuhr, as the Russians claim, but it is not godless as they suppose. Instead,

---

[1] DCNR. p. 214bc.
[2] And see David Wesley Soper, *Major Voices in American Theology* (Philadelphia: The Westminster Press, 1953), p. 47de.

the periodic overthrow of entrenched power is the work of God punishing nations for their sins. But whereas Communism had seen men as naturally good and the corrupting social evil as lying in a particular social structure, namely Capitalism, which only needed to be overthrown in order to usher in Utopia, Niebuhr, following Amos and the Prophetic tradition, claimed that it was the universally present sin in mankind that partly caused the creation and afterward caused the abuse of the oppressive power structures. The Russians saw the overthrow of the oppressive structure of Capitalism by means of the rise and revolt of the oppressed masses simply as the final dialectical movement within the dynamic structure of history. Amos had seen the overthrow of a nation in which social evil had become entrenched as God's punishment upon the sinful nation. This punishment Amos saw not as inflicted by the revolt of the oppressed within the nation but by a conquering foreign nation in the disaster of war. Later prophets declared that God's punishment would afterward overtake the conquering nation.[1] In line with Communism Niebuhr was able to say that social structures at the disposal of entrenched evil are headed for destruction. Contrary to Communism he could defy Communism's claim that it, as the avenger, was holy. This was because Niebuhr, in line with Amos and all the prophets, could see the evil not primarily in the particular social structure but in the inordinate greed of men for wealth and power even if they had to get it through oppressive or dishonest actions. The Communist party was not thought of as exempt from this sinful inner human drive for power or from the oppressive and unrighteous use of whatever power they had in order to get and keep more power. Communism like Capitalism therefore stood under the judgment of God and would eventually be punished by destruction. God is a

[1] Isaiah 10:12,15,16.

righteous God who demands righteousness from men, and God judges and punishes evil nations and societies.

The amazing thing about Niebuhr's return to the viewpoint of Amos was that he managed to do it and at the same time by-pass all the problems with which science confronted Orthodoxy and which Liberalism had only come to terms with by retreating to Pantheistic grounds. The problems all have to do with the question of miracle: How, in a situation in which the cause and effect sequences of the natural order seem unbroken, can there be any way to believe that a supernatural righteous God, who is completely outside (other than) the natural order, can feed his immediate personal influence at will into particular, chosen situations in the natural order, in order to assist in fulfilling the plan he has in mind for men? This is the great question that has played havoc with modern theology.

The idea of God as other than and supernatural to the creation has not meant for traditional Christianity the caricature of a bearded old man somewhere "off there" in the sky that some of the opponents of Orthodox Christianity have claimed to be its belief in order to discredit it. St. Paul, speaking of God said that he "gives[1] to all men life and breath and everything. And . . . he is not far from each one of us, for 'In him we live and move and have our being.' "[2] According to Augustine's claim, also, the power of God sustains all portions of the creation at all moments.[3] Whether or not the supernatural power of God sustains the creation makes no difference to scientific investigation. As science can only analyze the result of God's creating and sustaining power which is the universe, science is not in a position to pass judgment on the existence or non-existence of a Creator of the universe. If a Creator made and upholds nature in its standard routines of action, then the province of science is

---

[1] In the present tense.
[2] Acts 17:25,27,28.
[3] *The Confessions.* Bk. I, chaps. 2,3.

44

to discover those standard routines. This interrelation of the standard routines of nature's action *is* the nature that science knows and investigates. Whether or not these standard routines in nature are autonomous or not is not a question upon which science can pass judgment.

What science does claim, after painstaking study of nature, is that the routines, viewed from within nature, are apparently interrelated in an unbroken sequence of cause and effect within the natural order. The claim that miracle makes is that the supernatural God who made nature in its standard routines and upholds it constantly in its totality can sporadically at will feed into it here and there his direct personal influence in a new or non-constant fashion to further his own plans. If he did this, no violence would be done to nature's "laws." Nature would simply at some point be acted upon in an off schedule fashion by the God who made nature and upholds it in its standard routines. The expression "breaking the creation barrier" is used dramatically simply to emphasize God's off schedule activity in his creation. From God's point of view of course nothing peculiar or out of order or difficult would be involved. What would be fed into nature at any particular point in a miracle situation would be something other than the already standard routines of nature. But since what was new came direct from the self consistent God who made nature, it would do no violence to the already standard routines of nature but could easily be absorbed by them. That is to say, if God created miraculous bread and fishes for the five thousand to eat, that miraculous food could be digested and absorbed by the standard routines of natural digestive systems.

The crux of the problem, however, lies in the fact that if the special supernatural power of God were sporadically fed into nature, nature at those points would exhibit effects for which there were no *natural* causes, that is, no causes *within* the cause and effect sequences of the standard routines of nature's action. Viewed from within nature, as

45

scientific investigation must view and calculate things, there would appear to be events for which there were no causes. For these events would be due directly to a supernatural cause, namely God, and science cannot deal with the supernatural but only with what takes place within nature. If a miraculous event could be investigated by science it would appear as if an effect had taken place for which there was no cause within the standard routines that characterize the ongoing of nature. Thus it would appear to scientific investigation as if an event or effect had taken place for which there was no cause. From the scientific point of view, therefore, it would look as if a break had taken place in the total interrelated cause and effect sequences which characterize the ongoing of nature. The weight of accumulated scientific evidence is against breaks in the natural cause and effect sequences of nature.

Science could not really investigate to find out whether or not a miracle had occurred. For the method by which science makes its discoveries is the controlled experiment. According to this technique an experiment is repeated many times, and then repeated many times again with a slight change in some condition, such as temperature. In this way the particular routine in nature responsible for a particular occurrence can gradually be isolated. This technique would not work at all with respect to an occurrence dependent on the free choice of a Deity supernatural to nature.

William Temple, in his brilliant apology for the Christian faith has resolutely faced the issue of miracle and accepted miracle in his belief. His position is stated in *Nature, Man and God* (pp. 265ef, 267d-f, 269ab, 287e-288a, 293b-e, 295cd, 296d-297e, 302b-f),[1] and is in line with St. Augustine's description in the *Confessions* (Book I, chapters 2, 3, and 4; and Book VII, chapter 10) of God's active power and purpose relative to the world.[2] As the position

---

[1] William Temple, *Nature, Man and God* (London: Macmillan, 1951).

[2] Whitney J. Oates, editor, *The Basic Writings of St. Augustine* Volume I (New York: Random House, 1948) This volume includes the *Confessions*.

about miracle that I am trying to substantiate as essential to Christianity is that of Augustine and Temple, I have in Appendix A quoted the Temple passages and the passages from Book I of the *Confessions.* The passage from Book VII chapter 10 is the account of Augustine's first great vision of God and it is quoted and discussed at length together with pertinent passages from *Nature, Man and God* in my chapter on "Revelation."[1]

Miracle is the crucial point in the question of the relation of Christianity to science. As we shall see later, it is not usually the spectacular miracles like the stilling of the tempest that are absolutely essential to Christianity. The word "miracle" comes originally from the word meaning "to wonder," and so the word usually calls up in people's minds the thought of some highly spectacular wonder provoking occurrence in nature caused by the direct intervention of Deity. Educated people are embarrassed to admit a belief in such occurrences. However, it is not the spectacular quality of miracle, even where that exists, that is vital to Christianity. As will be seen later, where essential miracle takes place men are often unaware of its happening. What is essential for Christianity is that the God who made nature can sufficiently modify the cause and effect sequences of nature's standard routines to insert his influence at will directly into nature in a non-routine fashion. The question is, is nature impervious to penetration from without by a supernatural Deity, or can the God who made nature break the creation barrier and occasionally bring his influence directly to bear upon the creation which he has made?

Reinhold Niebuhr lines up with scientifically conditioned Liberalism in believing that the creation barrier cannot be broken.[2] It is his strong inner feeling that the ethical imperative is the surest clue to the nature of ultimate reality that keeps him from going over to a monistic philosophy.

---

[1] Chapter V. pp. 102-106.
[2] See *ante,* pp. 4-6, and CRPP. pp. 197f, 198a-c, 203a.

"The real difference," he says, "between naturalistic monism and dualistic supernaturalism is derived from ethical feeling."[1]

So anxious is Niebuhr not to seem to be a crude supernaturalist that a few of his statements seem to deny that God is supernatural at all. One of his early statements was that "philosophically competent scientists and scientifically competent philosophers . . . do not of course picture a God who is outside the world and at work upon it as a potter upon his clay."[2] Of course if God is not outside the world—meaning other than the world—Niebuhr's position is philosophically pantheistic, and that, as we have seen, would play havoc with the emphasis he puts on ethics. Actually this quotation may simply be an attempt to avoid charges of being crudely supernaturalistic. He was reacting violently against Liberalism, and he would be very anxious, as a young man with a great respect for the high intellectual calibre of Liberal scholarship, not to be thought of as going over to a reactionary theological position. His typical statements[3] make it obvious that he does believe in a supernatural God.

In analyzing Niebuhr's theology I am going on the assumption that he believes in a supernatural God.[4] The first enthusiastic and uncritical reading of Niebuhr certainly gives that impression; although upon critical re-reading it becomes obvious that he nowhere has a carefully developed exposition showing God to be supernatural. At points in his thinking where the issue could become acute he often makes his transition from one idea to the next in a spate of words whose meaning is not altogether clear. However, the whole nature of the religious piety of Niebuhr's writings as well as his ethical emphasis demand a belief in a supernatural God. Deny outright a supernatural righteous God and de-

---

[1] REE. p. 198de and see DCNR. p. 214 b-e.
[2] DCNR. pp. 210f-211b.
[3] Such as DST. p. 145a-e; CRPP. pp. 198bc, 203acd.
[4] FH. pp. 103e, 137c.

scribe God as a merely immanent force within nature and Niebuhr's whole prophetic message falls apart. What actually seems to happen is that Niebuhr believes in a supernatural righteous God in his personal piety and in his prophetic insight. In the metaphysical aspect of his teaching he is troubled by the heavy weight of scientifically conditioned philosophy against the supernaturalistic position. He never fully resolves the difficulty. If one accepts as part of Niebuhr's thought all the passages from the Bible, Augustine, and Luther which he quotes approvingly it is possible to put together selected passages to show that he is Orthodox. However, he will say enthusiastically that the Bible, Augustine, or Luther has said, or that the Church has claimed that such and such a thing is so. And then within a few pages he will throw in a sentence or paragraph which shows that he himself does not literally hold these beliefs. It is possible to put together a set of passages to show that he is sub-Christian in his personal beliefs. In Appendix C I have tried to list contrasting passages to show the inconsistencies between his reasoned thought and his spiritual longing. However, in my discussion throughout this book I am following the ideas that I believe to be basic to his religious and ethical message, and what is central to his message logically demands a belief in a supernatural and righteous God.

To return then to the question of Niebuhr's rediscovery of Amos. There is a whole side of Amos' thought that stresses cause and effect within the spiritual and social life. This does not mean that Amos if asked would have denied that God does break the creation barrier. Amos lived before there was an acute question of the relation of science to religion. He believed, for example, that God had sent drought, blight, mildew, locusts, and pestilence as a preliminary punishment upon the nation to warn it away from its sin.[1] Modern scholars would not take such a view of natural disasters. But this is not the main line of Amos' thought.

[1] Amos 4:7-10.

Arbitrarily leaving this and a few other of his passages out of consideration, Amos' central teaching develops the belief that there is cause and effect within the overall picture of the ongoing of society, and that throughout all nations the God who controls history[1] has built into his steady demand that men shall live righteously by their neighbors, the steady penalty that sin brings punishment and that a nation characterized by social injustice will be destroyed. It is typical of Amos' thought that this punitive destruction will be accomplished at the hands of an invading nation.[2] In Amos' own mind there seems to be the thought that God takes an active personal part in these occasional overthrowings of nations as a punishment for national injustice. "Does evil befall a city," he says, "unless the Lord has done it?"[3] However, one also finds embedded in his thought at least the first glimpse of the idea that God may have so universally ordained moral law for the governance of man that it is of necessity built into the structure of society, and any society that is not characterized by obedience to the moral law carries within it the weakness that eventually makes possible its final dissolution.[4] There are implications of this latter view in Amos in his initial woes against the nations. The formula in each of the eight instances is, "For three transgressions of" this nation "and for four, I will not revoke the punishment."[5] Here Amos may almost be interpreted to mean that since these nations have sinned the punishment is accordingly gathering momentum so that it would take a divine interference in the ongoing of society to stop the punishment. The clearest approximation to this point of view is Amos' third vision: "Behold, the Lord was standing beside a wall built with a plumb line, with a plumb line in his hand . . . and the sanctuaries of Israel shall be laid waste."[6] A

---

[1] Amos 1:3,6,9,11,13; 2:1,4,6,9; 3:1,2,6; 9:7.
[2] Amos 1:4,5,7,10,12,14,15; 2:2,3,5,14-16; 3:11; 4:2,3; 5:2,3,5.
[3] Amos 3:6.
[4] BT. p. 117de; FH. pp. 27f-28a.
[5] Amos 1, 2.
[6] Amos 7:7,9.

wall that is out of plumb will fall of its own weight: so a nation that is morally out of plumb has an inner insecurity that is a prelude to disaster.

Putting it in general terms one can say that the basic theme of Amos can be expressed in the words: Since God is righteous, sin brings punishment; therefore a nation that disobeys God's righteous demands for human justice in human relations will suffer disaster. Reinhold Niebuhr took this basic theme of Amos as the cornerstone of his theological-political thinking. "The wrath of God," Niebuhr says, "is the world in its essential structure reacting against the sinful corruptions of that structure."[1] It is hard to over-emphasize the importance of this theme as a religious rallying cry. Its strategic felicitousness lies in the fact that it is a return to Biblical religion which at the same time avoids all the basic difficulties that beset Liberalism.

We have seen that the central problem that Liberalism had tried to face was that of the implications for theology of man's growing knowledge, especially his scientific knowledge. If one held with generally accepted scientific theory that the cause and effect sequences within nature are unbroken one tended more and more to define God as immanent, with the resulting loss in confidence in God's righteousness that always accompanies Pantheism. But on this basic theme common to both Amos and Niebuhr one can philosophically imagine God as transcendent in a somewhat Deistic sense so that he never breaks the creation barrier and interferes with the cause and effect sequences within the natural order. But while holding this one can also hold that God is righteous and punishes sin. He can be thought to do this by making basic ethical standards so essentially a part of healthy social relations that a society that flagrantly flouts these standards undermines its own security and sows the seeds of its own destruction.[2] This comes about because the

---

[1] (2) HD. p. 56b and see (1) HN. p. 142ef and (2) HD. p. 71c.
[2] REE. pp. 121be, 122a, 126e.

. . . imperialistic effort is always self-defeating in the end. It arouses other forms of life to antagonism and creates resentments which finally become the instruments of its own undoing.[1]

Civilizations, like men and beasts, perish partly because they grow old and feeble and partly because they are slain by those whose enmity they have deserved by their ruthlessness.[2]

'Woe to thee,' declares the prophet Isaiah, 'that spoilest, and thou wast not spoiled; and dealest treacherously, and they dealt not treacherously with thee! when thou shalt cease to spoil, thou shalt be spoiled.' (Is. 33:1)[3]

[When the oligarch] finds his reign suffering from a loss of reverence and prestige he attempts to maintain it by sheer power. Thus he increases the injustices and exactions of his rule and multiplies the social resentments which will ultimately prove to be the engines of his undoing.[4]

History is as lenient as it is inexorable in its processes and is as slow in executing judgment as it is certain to pass a negative judgment upon predatory life. The chief instrument of judgment can be fashioned only by slow degrees. It is created by the resentments of the victims of injustice; and the burden bearers of the world are always inclined more to patience than to heroic rebellion.[5]

Although God does not break the creation barrier he can be thought of as genuinely effecting this punishment because it is due to the basic ethical "law" for social behavior which

---

[1] REE. p. 6e.
[2] REE. p. 31d.
[3] Quoted in (1)HN. p. 192b.
[4] REE. p. 34bc.
[5] REE. p. 51c-e.

is a divine law that man did not invent pragmatically but instead finds himself forced to take into account.

The second great problem that had gradually disintegrated Orthodoxy and had helped to steer many religious leaders toward the Liberal position was the growing religious uneasiness as to the righteousness of God if he condemned any soul to eternal hell for persistently flouting his authority and disregarding his moral law. These thoughtful Liberals did not want a saccharine God. On the other hand as we have seen, a God who was tough in the Orthodox sense in the eternal "no" he said to unrepentant sinners seemed to them immoral.

This issue is dodged by the Amos outlook which Niebuhr took over. There is no heaven or hell in Amos' teaching to raise the particular moral issue over hell which is involved in the Orthodox position. For Amos the whole moral drama was worked out within the earthly scene, and after this life there existed the at best shadowy existence of the grave. The confining of the human career to this life in Amos and other early Prophetic thought also eliminates the modern problem of consistency with science. To think of men as having a career after this life always involves the problem of the breaking of the creation barrier, because it describes a human being who is part of our universe as being taken out of our universe at death.[1]

While it would be wrong to say that for the early Hebrews man was ever "mass man" in exactly the modern sense of the term, it is nevertheless true that in the time of

---

[1] In trying to emphasize as strongly as possible that the wicked cannot escape God's judgment Amos does say in one place that God will reach man wherever he is in order to punish him, even if he fled to Sheol, to heaven, to the top of Carmel, or to the bottom of the sea. Amos 9:1-3. This is probably a sudden intuitive prophetic insight rather than a clearly defined constituent belief in Amos' general position, an instance of God pushing the prophet's thought beyond itself to the first hint in the Old Testament that God's power over and relationship to man extends beyond the grave. The idea is just thrown out and dropped and not taken up by succeeding prophets. It only comes into real focus in Hebrew thought six hundred years after Amos.

Amos God was thought of as dealing chiefly with the Hebrew nation as a whole rather than with the individuals within it. God was thought to punish or reward the nation, and individual men experienced disaster or welfare due to their having a relation to the life of the nation with which God was dealing. As the nation or tribe was thought of as the unit, if God visited the "iniquity of the fathers upon the children to the third and fourth generation" no injustice was thought to be done. The tribe had sinned in one generation and the tribe was punished in a succeeding generation. So God's justice was vindicated. Amos is thinking of rough justice in history in the large. Many perplexing problems are thereby eliminated.

Reinhold Niebuhr is most convincing when he, like Amos, is working with a focus upon the main outlines of history. Man, for the progression of his argument, is always mass man, rather than Tom, Dick, and Harry as individuals. His writings always have a doctrinaire quality even when dealing with the sin of individuals. This is true even when Niebuhr is talking about man's repentance in the confrontation of the Cross. It is a highly individual moment described in only general terms. That is, there is no consideration of the baffled floundering helplessness and pain in the human situation which is so often combined in a confused way with a sense of sin when an actual individual turns to the Cross in surrender to Christ. And there is no consideration of how, after once the human surrender to God has been made, God carries on from that point to assist the individual to an increasingly satisfactory relationship to himself. Dr. Niebuhr is so interested in man in the abstract that even his interest in Jesus seems to be largely an interest in him as a revelation of sacrificial love as such.[1] Of the human Jesus, in his day by day earthly career of a ministry of detailed love for those around him, and of what happened to him as an individual after he had performed the outstanding

---

[1] SDH. p. 232de; LNTC. p. 102a-d.

service to God of being at Calvary the perfect revelation of love, of all this that is so highly and poignantly individual, Niebuhr preserves a disconcerting silence. "In the New Testament the Atonement is the significant content of the Incarnation."[1] "The idea of the resurrection of the body can of course not be literally true."[2] ". . . The emancipation of an immortal soul from a mortal body (is) unthinkable."[3]

There was still another advantage in the retreat to Amos. It gave Niebuhr, and Protestant thought following his lead, a point of departure for a religious attack upon Communism. Communism claimed that the individualism of Christianity was selfish. It claimed that Western men were interested only in getting ahead themselves and had forgotten that each person is part of the mass of men and derives his safety from his relation to the mass. As Renaissance individualism had described man as autonomous, and had tended to make a man's enhancement of his own personality his chief goal, this Communistic charge had some truth in it; for in the so-called Western Christian countries Renaissance individualism had to a large extent supplanted the Christian individualism in which each individual is to be cherished because God wishes all men to become his adopted children and so united under him in brotherly love.

As against Communism's objection to current Western individualism Niebuhr, by returning to Amos, could now put forward a *Christian doctrine of God's relation to man in the mass*. This doctrine could show that God insists on social righteousness for the oppressed and punishes with destruction large groups, national and social, who exploit the weak. The terrifying message that the oppressing groups will some day be liquidated is thus seen to be common to both Communism[4] and Christianity.

Christianity could thus be shown to have in its heritage

---

1 (2)HD. p. 55c and see SDH. pp. 91de, 237a.
2 BT. p. 290b.
3 SDH. p. 237f.
4 REE. p. 127bc.

all that was best in Communism. Therefore Americans who were becoming alive to the social injustices of our industrial system did not have to go over to Communism in order to find an ideological basis for their practical demand for social righteousness. The ideological basis—with teeth in it—was already at hand in their Christian heritage.[1] Furthermore, the Communistic ideology could be shown to be based on a shaky foundation, namely the same naive trust in the natural goodness of man which is the shallow optimism of Rousseau that dominated Western thought in the eighteenth and nineteenth centuries and is now becoming discredited by the development of history.[2] Western Europe had believed that the social evils that harassed the little men were due to exploiting forms of social organization, to the entrenched powers of priesthood, nobility, and king.[3] If these exploiting forms of power were overthrown and all men were given the vote, the eighteenth and nineteenth centuries believed that the natural goodness of human nature would create a permanently good society. Now we are seeing that the evil in men's hearts can enable them to make use of the forms of democracy in the interests of a selfish exploitation of their fellow men.[4]

According to Niebuhr Communism is now making the same naive mistake of attributing evil primarily to an institution or form of entrenched power, in this case Capitalism.[5] Communism erroneously thinks that as soon as one form of oppression, namely Capitalism, is done away and a Communistic form of society set up in its place, that then there will be no further exploitation. Utopia will have arrived. What Communism fails to realize is that the sinful drive to power exists not in any institution, but in the human heart. Communism, like any other society, has to have some

---

[1] REE. p. 127bc.
[2] (1) HN. pp. 93a-94f.
[3] (1) HN. pp. 96e-97b.
[4] (1) HN. pp. 105a-106b.
[5] REE. p. 88bc.

form of organization and this always involves having some individuals with more than average power to assist in running the organization of society. These positions of power will be seized by people who crave power, or the positions will corrupt with a craving for power public spirited citizens who are put in office. The people who manage the power will eventually corrupt it into a means of exploiting others.[1] Thus Communism's claim that when once Communism has well established itself permanent Utopia will have arrived can be seen to be a mistaken prophecy.

At one blow Reinhold Niebuhr had cut the Gordian knot. He had made it clear that the best in Communistic ideology can be found in Christianity. He had put his finger on a vital weakness in Communistic ideology in an area where it differs from Christianity to show that the Communistic claim that they are ushering in the perfect society, caring for the welfare of all alike, is an illusion. He therefore showed Christianity to be more realistic than Communism. He broke away from the saccharine and sentimentalized picture of God popularly preached by Liberalism, and he replaced the picture by a conception of a righteous God who demands social righteousness and is tough in his implementing of these demands. Yet all this was done by Niebuhr without any need for a description of God as breaking the creation barrier to obtain his ends. So Niebuhr's religious theory at this point does not need to run into any difficulties on the score of the relation of religion to science. Furthermore, by making the righteousness of God the point of departure in his thinking, Niebuhr escapes the Pantheistic trap in which Liberalism tends to fall with its increasingly immanent description of God. Niebuhr's God in no way interferes with the ongoing of creation according to unbroken scientific procedures. And yet his God is transcendent to the world and watches over it and vigorously demands—with penalties for disobedience—that men shall

---

[1] CPP. pp. 192a-194d.

live socially righteous lives. For practical purposes Reinhold Niebuhr's religious thought is a kind of Prophetic Deism.

And in spite of the toughness of the big stick with which God punishes sin Niebuhr also manages to eliminate completely that other stumbling block in Orthodoxy which was troubling the tenderest consciences of twentieth century Christianity. He eliminates hell completely. God can be tough in relation to human sin and yet not use hell to fulfill his punishment. The reason Niebuhr can emphasize righteousness and at the same time eliminate the problem of hell completely is that in his return to Amos he has returned to a conception of God dealing with societies in the mass, not with people as individuals. Since the age of any society is not limited to the three score years and ten there is always time for retributive disaster to overtake societies on this earth.

And all this was accomplished by Reinhold Niebuhr by a return to the Bible and by interpreting the Bible at face value. This also helps explain Niebuhr's popularity with the educated laity. They had too much knowledge of science to be content with a Fundamentalist type of religion. And yet there has been an inarticulate longing on the part of many for a return to Biblical religion. The average intelligent layman is a little uneasy with the subtleties of modern theologies. He is simply confused when theologians claim to make Christianity understandable and then imply that although they use the word "God" they redefine it, so that what they mean by it is neither the Giver of the Law on Mt. Sinai nor the heavenly Father of our Lord Jesus Christ. The layman is disturbed when the theologians tell him that they believe in the redemption of the world by Christ's death and Resurrection and then admit that they do not take the accounts in the Gospel's and Paul's letters with anything approaching literalness, but assume that the New Testament accounts are mythological expressions, embroidered by the early Church in the course of its teaching far beyond the actual facts of the career of Jesus Christ. The layman is disturbed for example, when he finds that according to modern theologians the Resurrection turns out to be not a literal rising from the dead on the first Easter but a mythological expression meaning only the influence of the thoughts about Christ that live on in our memories.

This worries the layman. Not having the benefit of a theological education he is inclined to feel that if the major claims of the New Testament are not literally true in a historical sense, then Christianity is a religion built upon error, a religion that would be wonderful if true but unfortunately it is not true.

But in Reinhold Niebuhr's return to Amos there is no theological double talk. In the selective use that Niebuhr makes of Amos' message he takes the general sense literally, and if Amos could read Niebuhr's exposition of God's relation to history Amos would approve of his teaching. The importance of Niebuhr's return to Amos can scarcely be overemphasized.

CHAPTER IV

THE NATURE OF MAN'S SIN AND ITS
IMPLICATION FOR THE CHARACTER OF GOD

BUT THE DEVELOPMENT of Hebrew Prophetic thought did
not stop with Amos. He was followed by Hosea. And Reinhold Niebuhr's thinking is far more complicated than one
would guess from the isolation of one basic strand of it in
the previous chapter.

It is a moot point as to whether Amos teaches at all the
idea of the love of God. He does not emphasize it directly
although some have argued that it is implied in the fact that
God punishes sin. If God did not care for or love men, it
can be argued, he would not be annoyed when the poor are
oppressed. However, it is agreed that the prophetic teaching of Amos is on the level of righteousness rather than of
love, and because it is on the level of righteousness God can
be thought of in terms of a conscientious administrator who
deals with men in the mass and seeks the overall well being
of a group. So far, therefore, as Niebuhr is speaking in
terms of the message of Amos he is justified in speaking only
of man in the mass. But as soon as one begins to talk about
love one has to talk about the personal relation of one
individual to another. For love involves the personal relationship of individuals. It is not a mass affair.

It was Hosea's great message that God is a God of love
as well as of justice. It is true that Hosea thought of God's
relation to Israel in the same collective terms that had characterized the teaching of Amos: God relates himself to the
nation which he appropriately rewards or punishes; individ-

60

ual men therefore receive bane or blessing from God *via* their relation to the state. The question of bad individuals experiencing good fortune when God favored the state, and of good individuals receiving ill fortune when God punished the state, involved the moral problem of God's relation to the individual, and that was a religious question that had not yet in Hosea's time arisen above the horizon of men's spiritual consciousness. It was enough if God dealt righteously with the state *en masse*.

But now Hosea added to Amos' message that God dealt righteously with nations as totalities the further thought that God loved Israel as a nation. And yet one does not love in the mass. One loves individuals. Love is by definition a relationship between individuals. So Hosea, trying to convince Israel that God loves the nation, has to personify the nation and speak of her under figurative terms that are highly personal. In the vivid and extended marriage metaphor[1] Hosea says that God loves the erring nation as a husband might love a faithless wife and buy her back into his household and protect her after he had discarded her for committing adultery.[2] As a figurative comparison Hosea had chosen the most intensely personal of human relationships and the human relationship that is emotionally most highly charged. If God loved the nation *en masse as if* a man were loving his erring wife, it was inevitable that Hebrew prophetic thought would some day come to see that God loves individual human beings. Jeremiah's prophecy of the New Covenant[3] and Ezekiel's claim that men are not punished for the sins of their fathers but are rewarded or punished for their own individual deeds[4] are in line with the growing emphasis upon individuality. So, too, is Ezekiel's description of God as the shepherd of Israel who seeks the lost, brings

---

[1] Hosea 1:1-3:5.
[2] There are other modern interpretations of Hosea's marriage figure, but this through the centuries has been the standard interpretation.
[3] Jeremiah 31:27-34.
[4] Ezekiel 18.

back the strayed, binds up the crippled, and strengthens the weak.[1] Jesus is the culmination of this line of direction in Prophetic thought as is seen in his claim that God is the heavenly Father, who has numbered the hairs of our heads, knows what we need before we ask him, searches for sinners as a shepherd for his lost sheep, and rewards even those who offer one of these little ones a cup of cold water.[2]

The idea of God's love for individuals came into focus slowly in Hebrew thought.[3] It is that thought's culmination rather than its starting point. Because the Hebrews thought first in terms of God's love for the nation it is easy to fall into the error of thinking that God—or human beings—love the large group, the society, first, and love individuals secondarily. But this is not true to the way people actually love. It is the nature of love that it shall be the relation of one individual to another. A nation or a social class as an abstraction cannot be loved.[4] All that can be loved are the individuals included in the group that is designated by the abstraction. This point is of vital importance to twentieth century religious thinking and needs to be made perfectly clear.

One word of caution must be given. The word love is used with many definitions in the twentieth century and not all the definitions are Christian. There are attempts to make love into a great cosmic force and so depersonalize it. A good deal of poetry hovers in a borderline area between a Christian and a non-Christian definition of love. When people talk about two great forces in the world, love and hate, they sometimes speak as if love consists of all that makes immediately for beauty and serenity and harmony, and as if hate includes all that makes immediately for lack

---

[1] Ezekiel 34:14-16.

[2] Matthew 6:8; 10:30,42; Luke 15:3-6.

[3] The conception received strong early support from the life of Jeremiah.

[4] When Niebuhr is speaking politically he is very much aware that love is a specifically personal matter. See MMIS. pp. 53d-54c and FH. pp. 184a-185d.

of harmony. And they imply that in the sub-human world love is all that makes for harmony, like the happy sunlight causing the flowers to grow in the meadow. And they imply that hate is all that makes for disharmony like the unleashed violence of earthquakes, tidal waves, and volcanoes. This is really closer to the Taoist principle of Yin and Yang than it is to the Hebraic-Christian idea of love.

It is interesting to notice that with the twentieth century loss by Western civilization of a belief in a supernatural righteous God, with the consequent debasing of the definition of the Moral Law to *mores,* something merely relative and pragmatic, there has been a growing tendency to debase the Christian ideal of love to the ideal of non-moral social harmony considered as an end in itself. Popular parlance is beginning to substitute the non-moral conception of "togetherness" for love. Togetherness is a materialistic not a spiritual term, and can be applied to non-conscious nature, for example, to peas in a pod.

Love in the Hebraic-Christian sense is always righteous love. In the Hebraic-Christian sense love is always a particular self desiring to have communion with another self, having respect for the integrity of the other self's individuality, and taking practical steps both to practise outgoing concern for the welfare of the other self and to obtain communion with the other self. Since righteousness concerns detailed actions to assist in insuring the integrity of other selves and their welfare, love can be said to complete and crown righteousness in human experience, and to summarize righteousness in the heart of God. Therefore aspects of nature that are not conscious cannot be said to love, for the moral law does not apply to the lower orders of nature which have no consciousness at all or only rudimentary consciousness. Furthermore, even at the human level any description of love merely in terms of the force or power making for immediate beauty and harmony is inadequate from the Jewish-Christian point of view because it blurs moral distinctions. For it might call the harmony and beauty of a tastefully furnished home "good" without considering whether the money that made possible the beauty was honestly earned. And it might label as a disrupting influence and therefore as "bad" the disconcerting activity of Amos, disturbing the surface serenity of the immediate social situation in the interests of righteousness.

Using love in the Hebraic-Christian sense it is an illusion to think that one could love directly masses of men, such as states or classes, instead of loving primarily individual men.[1] When one speaks primarily of loving one's nation what one is really doing is loving some contemporary individuals within the nation, and some of its individual citizens of past generations. For whatever may be people's theories against the possibility of life after death the world has always emotionally felt that its dead are not wholly dead as long as the larger social group to which their lives contributed still survives. To the extent to which the social situation of the present prolongs the social situation of the past the beloved dead who contributed to the social situation of the past are emotionally felt to be to a slight extent still a living part of the present social situation. If a society or nation is destroyed, the honored dead whose memory the nation was guarding seem to have died fully. The passion to preserve a nation turns out on closer inspection to be a passion for preserving individual lives. If we love those in the past whom we have not seen, we do it because their influence has penetrated into our lives and into the lives of individuals who are our contemporaries and whom we love. So our love for our ancestors and for the heroes of the past is an aspect of our love for ourselves and our friends. If we love those of our contemporaries whom we have not seen, such as people of other races on the other side of the world, we do it by projecting upon them in imagination the love we have felt for individuals whom we have known personally.[2]

---

[1] DCNR. pp. 126d, 128a-e.
[2] In this regard see I John 4:20.

One loves one's nation in the abstract because one sees the nation as the setting for the individuals one loves, and then by imagination one projects one's love for these known individuals to include by spiritual analogy all the people of the nation that forms the society in which they live. Loyalty is love in action.

Reinhold Niebuhr recognizes that the sensitive moral consciousness flourishes most adequately under the inspiration of personal love which expresses itself as loyalty, and that this is a major ingredient in patriotism. He says:

> The religious conscience is sensitive not only because its imperfections are judged in the light of the absolute but because its obligations are felt to be obligations toward a person. The holy will is a personal will. . . . Moral attitudes always develop most sensitively in person-to-person relationships. That is one reason why more inclusive loyalties, naturally more abstract than immediate ones, lose some of their power over the human heart; and why a shrewd society attempts to restore that power by making a person the symbol of the community. The exploitation of the symbolic significance of monarchy, after it has lost its essential power, as in British politics for instance, is a significant case in point. The king is a useful symbol for the nation because it is easier for the simple imagination to conceive a sense of loyalty toward him than toward the nation. The nation is an abstraction which cannot be grasped if fitting symbols are not supplied. A living person is the most useful and potent symbol for this purpose.[1]

There is also a great deal of self-love in patriotism. A frantic patriotism is sometimes a panicked fear for one's personal safety. But of course, one's self is an individual, and if one loves the nation out of self-love the love of the nation or of society in the mass is built upon a foundation

---

[1] MMIS. pp. 53d-54c.

of love for an individual, namely one's self. "A man's devotion to his community always means the expression of a transferred egoism as well as of altruism."[1] And one's love for one's nation as the guardian of one's self can refer to something more than the preserving of one's physical life. Patriotic devotion is greatly stimulated by one's realization that one's achievements and one's loved ones and the culture that are part of one's self are guarded by one's nation.

It may be objected that this is an inadequate description of patriotism because it leaves out the real devotion, which is a quasi-love, that people have for the actual soil of the land that has fed them and been to them from childhood a kind of nursing mother. However, even here the land is loved because of its relation to one's self, family, and friends and to the culture which is part of one's self. This again is one's love for individuals. In fighting to preserve the soil of one's native land one is not practising outgoing love toward the soil as such to protect it. For whatever nation possesses the soil is immaterial to any consciousness or any welfare of the soil itself. Under varying social and national vicissitudes the soil continues there unharmed.

So many personal interests and so many beloved individuals may be guarded by the nation that a man may sacrifice his life and property and the life of a loved one to the nation, but the love that he has for the nation is built upon the foundation of love for individuals.

The nature of the relation of love for the individual to love for the group and the primacy of the former can be seen more clearly if we take as an illustration something simpler than patriotism. It is possible for men to some extent to love animals because they can practise outgoing helpful concern for the individual animals they domesticate, and the animals in turn can feel and show some affection for men. For example, Syrian shepherds are said really to love their sheep. With a flock of one hundred sheep a man can

---

[1] MMIS. p. 40e.

know each animal by name[1] and be alert to each animal's particular needs.[2] The shepherd does not love the flock as such, as an impersonal aggregate. He loves the flock as a flock because it is composed of members that he has watched over individually. The probabilities are that one of our Western ranchers, with a "band" of two thousand sheep in his care,[3] would not be able to love his "band" in a sense really comparable to the love of the Syrian shepherd. This is because he would have to deal with the sheep in the mass, rather than as individuals. If a Western rancher could be said really to love his "band" it would be because there might be two or three sheep of which he had made personal pets,[4] and with these pet sheep and with the occasional sheep he had individually helped he could establish a slight degree of communion and fellowship which he could then imaginatively project to include the band as a whole. But although a man might therefore be said to feel love for a band of two thousand sheep, no man ever felt love for a colony of eighty thousand bees. This is because in caring for them he can deal with them only in the mass, not with individual bees. He has never made a pet of any particular bee and established a personal fellowship and communion with it which he can then imaginatively project to include love for the whole hive.

It is not an accident that that further development of Judaism which became Christianity emphasized God's saving care for the individual. It is implicit in the claim that God is loving because it is of the basic nature of love to care for individuals. In all Christian-Jewish thought God is

---

[1] Luke 15:4; John 10:3,4.

[2] See Luke 15:3-7; Psalm 23; and William Allen Knight, *The Song of Our Syrian Guest* (New York: The Pilgrim Press, 1906); Isaiah 40:11; Ezekiel 34:2-5, 11-16. *The Interpreter's Bible,* Vol. VIII (New York: Abingdon Press, 1955) commenting on Luke 15:4 says, "A hundred sheep would constitute a large flock in the Palestine of Jesus' day."

[3] John Gunther, *Inside U.S.A.* (New York: Harper and Brothers, 1947), pp. 137, 138.

[4] II Samuel 12:1-6.

67

the same yesterday, today, and forever. The idea that God existed lovelessly for a large part of his existence and then rather late thought up the love relationship for the first time is inconsistent with Biblical religion. This means that the Hebrew God was always a God of love, loving primarily the individuals composing the nation and loving only secondarily the more abstract nation that they composed. This would have to be so because this is the nature of love. *However, the love of God was revealed to Israel in reverse order,* first as love of the nation and later as love for the individuals in the nation.

When Amos thought of God as righteous he thought of the great sin as social injustice. But when Hosea saw that God deeply loved the nation he shifted the emphasis upon sin to the sin of Baalism, personal disloyalty to the God of Israel by the sin of worshipping other gods. The shift is not by chance. For if love is basic to the character of God, then the basic sin against God is disloyalty, because disloyalty is the basic sin against love. And worshipping other gods is disloyalty to the loving God. The reason Christianity has described the basic sin as pride is that pride is giving one's basic loyalty to one's self and one's desires, and this is a form of idolatry and a disloyalty to the loving God.

On the subject of God's relation to man's collective social injustice and of God's relation to social and national disaster Reinhold Niebuhr took his stand with Amos. But his religious position does not stop with that of Amos. Much of Reinhold Niebuhr's creative work has been in the area of tracing the antecedents of the sin of social injustice. He finds man's constant problem to lie in his insecurity. To offset his insecurity man seeks the aggrandizement of his own personality by power, wealth, prestige, and knowledge. But in his feverish desire for security he seeks these things inordinately, beyond the permission of God. Men try to make themselves the center of the universe. Their creatureli-

68

ness is in itself no sin but man should keep it in its proper place in obedient dependence upon God. If man did this and in constant loyalty to God put God's wishes first, man would accept his own creatureliness and his social actions would then keep their proper bounds of obedience to God's right-eous Law, and sin and evil would not be built into society as they actually are in history. Niebuhr traces exhaustively the stages by which "each person is tempted when he is lured and enticed by his own desire. Then desire when it has conceived gives birth to sin; and sin when it is full-grown brings forth death."[1] The social injustice to which Niebuhr has traced the downfall of nations has its genesis in men's sinful pride, refusing to accept the bounds of creatureliness set for them by God, but instead under the pressure of the fear which their insecurity engenders pushing their self as-sertion to unrighteous extremes that bring hardship and injustice upon their fellow men.

There is a threefold reason why Niebuhr is so anxious to trace social sin back to man's self-idolatry and rebellion against God. In the first place this is the traditional Christian interpretation of social evil. All the specific social sins are traced back to the sin of pride which is self-idolatry and disobedience to the loving God and so disloyalty to God. In the second place, this traditional approach to the prob-lem plays into Niebuhr's constant anti-Communist polemic. Communism, ideologically, is largely staked on the claim that a particular institution, namely Capitalism, is oppressing the workers, and that once this institution is liquidated the naturally good human nature will make it possible for men to live together in peace, without oppression. Niebuhr's claim is that the whole race is a fallen race because when choice is presented to each individual, men always put their own desires ahead of loving God with all their heart, soul, strength, and mind, and their neighbors as themselves. Men are themselves corrupt and therefore will corrupt and ex-

---

[1] James 1:14, 15.

ploit for their own advantage any social framework under which they live. Therefore Communism's confidence that its own political society is the final solution to the problem of history and that it will usher in Utopia is an illusion.

The third reason for Niebuhr's emphasis upon sin as basically man's disloyal rebellion against God is his desire as a Christian preacher to wake America out of its complacency. The little dishonesties, the little oppressions, the small use of collective power, obtained through loyalty to one's group, in the interests of maneuvering for one's own advantage without thought for the welfare of others outside the group, these are things that all men do due to the drive of their own insecurity. They are done by nice people who are decent citizens and who do not flagrantly disobey the moral code. But the snowballing effect of the trivial illegitimate pressures men bring to bear upon others to get their own way becomes built into society, and undermines its strength.[1]

In his polemic against the sin of "nice people," the pillars of society, Niebuhr emphasizes that there must be more than the keeping of the law codes of decent behavior. For selfish human ingenuity can and does "learn the ropes" of the moral law codes and then, while working within their technical requirements, uses the prestige and stability that they give to enhancing its own power which is governed by the desire for selfish self-aggrandizement; and this line of action gradually works hardship upon those weak enough to be exploited. For Niebuhr a person's actions should be governed not only by the general rules of decent behavior but also by love which is affectionate concern outgoing into practical action for the welfare of others and for personal communion with them. This type of concern does not exploit others as "things" to minister to one's own welfare, but respects them as individual personalities and wishes the communion of spiritual fellowship with them.

---

[1] DCNR. pp. 132e-133f.

Now if the basic nature of sin is defined as disloyal rebellion against God, certain implicit corollaries follow as to the nature of God. Why, for instance, should rebellion against God be sinful? It is not so considered in all religions. In the *Bhagavad-Gita*'s summary of Hindu spiritual teaching an attempted rebellion against deity, Brahman, or lack of consideration for Brahman would not be considered sinful. It would merely be considered unenlightened. And in our own Western civilization not all rebellion is considered sinful. In fact we often think of rebellion against oppression as virtuous. In our total life outlook if we think of the controlling power of the universe as the blind crushing force of matter then we agree with Bertrand Russell that man's rebellion against this controlling power in the name of human intelligence, decency, and value is a virtue, even if the rebellion must be short lived and is doomed to eventual failure. The reason why Hinduism would not consider an attempted rebellion against Brahman as sinful is that Brahman is non-moral and non-loving. To sin against a person involves a disloyalty to the person. Disloyalty to the person is a sin against righteous love. When one sins against a person or against God, one is in an *un*ethical relation to the person or God, and one cannot be in an *un*ethical relation to that to which it would be impossible to be in an *ethical* relation. But the Brahman of Hinduism is non-moral and non-loving and so has no ethical relationships with anyone. This is why a man in a state of attempted rebellion against Brahman would not be considered sinful. The word "sin" would be meaningless.

In Christianity on the other hand, the thing that makes man's rebellion against God sinful is that God is righteous-loving. By definition, to be righteous-loving involves being governed by outgoing concern in practical action for the welfare of other individuals and for personal communion with them. It is because God loves men that disloyalty to him is sin. Niebuhr's theology is built upon the belief in the righteousness of God, and Niebuhr believes that righteousness at its height is love.[1] He says that "The highest justice of God is the holiness of His love. It is love as law which man affronts and defies."[2]

But if God's nature is really characterized by righteous love then he really desires spiritual communion with individual men and actively works for the welfare of individual men. "Personality exhibits itself supremely in purposes of fellowship or love."[3] But if God had communion with individual men, then, since he is a supernatural God (as he has to be if he is to be thought of as righteous) he is the Creator of men, and man is a creature and so a part of created nature. If the supernatural Creator had personal communion with an individual who is within the creation then at that point the creation barrier would be broken and in this act of communion the Supernatural would influence nature in an off-schedule or non-routine way. At the point of communion an extra-natural influence would influence nature. Another way of showing the same difficulty is to point out that if God loves an individual man he must take practical steps for the man's welfare, and to do that would mean acting toward a particular thing in the natural order in a particular way, which would involve something more than the standard routines of actions which God constantly upholds in nature as a whole. In other words, taking any special practical steps for a particular man's welfare (such as guiding or strengthening him) would involve breaking the creation barrier. This is why it is impossible to describe a Deistic God as loving. As Deistic he does not interact with nature at will and so cannot have communion with men who are part of nature. *But to be governed by a desire for the welfare of others and for communion with them and to act practically in relation to other individuals to attain this end is righteous*

---

[1] (2) HD. pp. 246cd, 247a-d, 248a, 251b-252c.

[2] (2) HD. p. 56e.

[3] William Temple, *Nature, Man and God* (London: Macmillan, 1951), p. 263c.

love by definition. The belief that God is righteous-loving cannot consistently be held without belief in miracle.

But Niebuhr follows the usual scientifically conditioned thought of the twentieth century in not admitting that the standard order of nature can be penetrated from without. Very well then, if God does not commune helpfully with men he does not love men. So if God is not characterized by active loving concern (which has to be implemented by practical action in order to be loving concern) for a man's welfare the man is not disloyal to God's love when he rebels against God. So the man's rebellion against God is not sin and the subtle analysis of sin as man's rebellion against God's love, for which Reinhold Niebuhr is so justly famous, will not hold. We have seen that in Hinduism there is no doctrine of sin in the Christian sense because there is no loving God to whom to be disloyal. Love is an active interpersonal relationship. If God does not have active interpersonal relationships then in Christianity there is no *loving* God to whom man can be disloyal, and so, as in Hinduism, the Christian could not be said to sin by being disloyal to God.

As long as Niebuhr is arguing from Amos' position he can speak of man in the mass and man's sin merely as social injustice, and he can make a good case for the righteous God punishing sinful nations, and make it while still declining to admit that nature can be supernaturally penetrated. Just as soon, however, as Niebuhr analyses sin as disloyalty to God he brings love into the description of God, and God cannot be described as loving without implying that he can break the creation barrier. One cannot have it both ways. Inconsistency threatens Niebuhr's thought at its center, not on its periphery. Niebuhr is aware of this problem and tries to get around it. He refers respectfully to ancient Christian writers who *did* believe that God breaks the creation barrier. When he is speaking in terms of his own beliefs he tries to give the impression that God is genuinely active toward individual men, and genuinely does things to and for them.

73

But the wording when analyzed turns out not to genuinely admit that God breaks the creation barrier. An example of this is the previously quoted passage[1] in which Niebuhr is describing the British political astuteness in keeping the monarchy, because it is easier for people to loyally love a personal sovereign than it is the nation as an abstraction. Niebuhr continues:

> In religion all the higher moral obligations, which are lost in abstractions on the historic level, are felt as obligations to the supreme person. Thus both the personality and the holiness of God provide the religious man with a reinforcement of his moral will and a restraint upon his will-to-power.[2]

People who actually believe that God breaks the creation barrier could legitimately use this statement upon occasion. But writing such as Niebuhr's that does not commit itself beyond such statements as this is not admitting that this can happen. Upon analysis, and taken in conjunction with the immediately preceding statement that the British king is a symbol, all that the quotation from Niebuhr admits is that (a) men *have ideas* in their minds that God is personal and God is holy; (b) *these ideas in a man's mind furnish the man with a strong incentive* to be morally good and to restrain his will-to-power; (c) ideas that furnish men with strong incentives (and this could include mistaken ideas) have a genuine effect upon men's actions. In the quotation it is only the man that is described as an *active power*. No action on God's part relative to man is stated. There is no description of "grace" as "power" helping man to reinforce his moral will and restrain his will-to-power. The foregoing analysis may seem to be hair-splitting. But it is valid because this instance is typical of all Niebuhr's writing. Niebuhr's inability to describe divine "grace" as Divine Power

---

[1] *Ante*, p. 65.
[2] MMIS. p. 54cd.

74

impinging upon human life is all of a piece with his inability to have an adequate doctrine of the Holy Spirit. And both inabilities stem from his inability to believe that God breaks the creation barrier.

Niebuhr tries to show that God is loving and that his grace helps men. His *acts* of grace, however, turn out to be his "uncovenanted mercies" and divine grace making the sun rise upon the evil and the good and his sending rain on the just and the unjust,[1] or the periodic overflow of the Nile River which is "a special gift of grace" to Egypt.[2] Also in nations' "glory, when the disintegration of evil is already apparent in their life and yet ultimate destruction is so long postponed, their fate reveals the 'longsuffering' of the divine mercy."[3] "It is a literal fact that the processes of nature and history are revelations of grace as well as of judgment."[4] Niebuhr also sees it as an example of God's grace that the welfare of the ruled and of the rulers sometimes coincide so that in spite of the rulers' human sinfulness they do right, because the thing that enhances their own prestige and security makes for the welfare of those they govern. He calls this a " 'righteousness which is not our own,' this virtue by grace of providence and coincidence."[5]

But these are all very general routine types of grace built in, as it were, to the structure of the creation. And Niebuhr regularly speaks of God's love and grace toward *man,* using the collective expression, rather than God's grace to individual men. It is true that the devout will see God's graciousness in the beneficence of nature and the fortunate periods of history. But the skeptical thought will intrude: If this is the only way God's grace shows itself is it not just a pious way of saying that the laws governing nature and the social order are so constituted that rain will fall indiscriminately,

---

[1] IAH. p. 50ab, Matthew 5:45; REE. pp. 282b, 286bc.
[2] DST. pp. 60ef, 61ab. See also (1)HN. p. 190bc, and Ezekiel 29:3; 30:8,12.
[3] (2)HD. p. 305f.
[4] REE. p. 285e.
[5] FH. p. 222bcd.

that rivers will overflow periodically, that cause and effect on a large social scale is slow, and that the welfare of the rulers and the ruled do, as a matter of fact, coincide in large areas of their activity? Like the general Christmas greeting printed in a newspaper, this description of grace (involving no breaking of the creation barrier) leaves us longing for a personal touch.

In modern literature and in magazine articles on the psychology of human relations the theme has been worn threadbare of the inadequacy of those homes in which either the husband is merely a "good provider" of physical comforts for his wife, ignoring her need for spiritual companionship, or the parents are merely "good providers" for their children but take no sympathetic thought for their personal problems or need of understanding adult companionship. Members in such homes suffer emotionally from lack of love. In the same way a God who was merely a "good provider" causing his sun to rise and his rain to fall and his Nile to overflow its banks would be lacking as a loving God because to love truly includes desiring communion with the individual loved. If human beings did not sin by disloyalty to God but instead loyally responded to his love by loving him with all their heart, soul, strength, and mind and their neighbor as themselves (as Niebuhr's ethic has to demand that they should do), their love for him would, by the definition of love, desire communion with him who is the object of their love. It is this state rather than the state of sin for which man was created. If God should love men and men should love God, there would exist a mutual desire for communion between them because that desire is a basic characteristic of love. And it is true that sinful though men are the most deeply pious souls in the world have always desired communion with God more than any physical gift or any gift of fortune that he can give them.

But since God to be a God of love in the Jewish-Christian sense must also be a God of righteousness, he must be a supernatural and not a pantheistic God. He must be *other than* the creation which includes man. So if the supernatural God has any communion with men or if men have any communion with the supernatural God there is intercourse across nature's outer boundaries and the creation barrier is broken. As we have seen Niebuhr considers science an authority about nature and concedes that science has established that nature is not open to penetration from without.[1]

Niebuhr is thus in the difficult position of having no intellectual grounds for believing that there can be communion between God and men. This is why his teaching is so lacking on the side of constructive positive description of the Christian life. He talks in general about God's relation to man. But man is an abstraction. If God is going to have human relationships it must be with *men*. By taking Christ's great love commandment seriously[2] Niebuhr implies that man was made for harmony with God but when man fell the image of God was defaced in him and he was estranged from God. Since all men fall when choices are presented to them,[3] the harmony with God is merely hypothetical of what would have happened if man had not universally fallen.[4] It is what would have transpired regularly if the race had not sinned. A merely unrealized possibility does not raise the issue of breaking the creation barrier. And even had man realized this ideal relation to God, the word Niebuhr uses for this ideal relationship is "harmony,"[5] which is a static word, lacking the motion of spiritual interaction contained in the word "communion." Furthermore Niebuhr, as we shall later see, lacks both a vivid doctrine of the Holy Spirit and a genuine belief in the Incarnation, and so he does not describe Christ's Atonement as reestablishing communion of God with man across the creation barrier.

Because man sinned and the image of God was defaced

---

[1] See, *ante,* references on pp. 4-6.
[2] Mark 12:30; (1)HN. p. 286b-d.
[3] (1)HN. pp. 276-280.
[4] (1)HN. p. 287ab.
[5] (1)HN. p. 286d.

in him he is cut off from God and his understanding of God is darkened. But his understanding is not completely darkened for then the ignorance that he claims in order to justify his choices in the direction of self aggrandizement would be wholly innocent ignorance.

If the human race's vision was darkened by sin and if God loves men it would be logical to suppose that he would try to reveal himself to them. This Niebuhr claims that God does do. Niebuhr makes a great point of the fact that outside of the Jewish-Christian religion all religions are manmade, what man has thought up about God. Only in the Jewish-Christian religion do we have a religion of God taking the initiative and revealing himself to man.[1] We must now ask ourselves in some detail how Niebuhr believes the revelation to take place and whether or not he describes God as breaking the creation barrier in the course of revealing himself to men.

---

[1] Niebuhr's discussion consistently avoids Islam.

CHAPTER V

GOD'S LACK OF ASSISTANCE TO MEN: REVELATION

IF SPIRITUAL COMMUNION did take place in the relation of a man to God it would involve a breaking of the creation barrier by Deity and a conscious specific insertion of divine influence into the creation at unpredictable intervals which would modify the course of nature by a tinkering with the creation, of which man is a part, by a Power from beyond nature, and thus break the closed system of causality as seen from within nature. If the Lord actually instructed Paul in a vision at Corinth, "Do not be afraid, but speak and do not be silent; for I am with you, and no man shall attack you to harm you; for I have many people in this city,"[1] and if as a result Paul "stayed a year and six months, teaching the word of God to them,"[2] you have an instance of God's breaking the creation barrier, that is, miracle. If in this instance, and in all other comparable instances in the book of Acts, all that you have is Paul's knowledge of what Jesus' followers said about him, plus Paul's personal knowledge of the Corinthian situation, plus the unpredictable activity of Paul's subconscious mind, you do not have a breaking of the creation barrier and miracle, but you have denied the validity of New Testament Christianity.

If this divine breaking of the creation barrier can occur, there is no implication that physical laws have been "broken." For this penetration into nature is the work of the self-

---

[1] Acts 18:9,10.
[2] Acts 18:11.

79

consistent Power who ordered natural law in the first place and constantly sustains nature under it. But what is implied is that the order of natural law, as seen from within nature, is not a closed system but that nature can be penetrated and modified at will by a conscious designing Power that is outside of nature.

The problem is not just an academic issue but a question that faces us in our daily lives. If one holds that the creation barrier is never broken one is denying the validity of all prayer except perhaps the prayer of adoration. If one thinks one's self superior to Jesus' crudely petitionary prayers, "Give us this day our daily bread,"[1] and "Abba, Father, all things are possible to thee; remove this cup from me,"[2] and if one thinks one prays only for spiritual blessings, one has still not removed the difficulty.

If a man faced a difficult decision and could not make up his mind which of two alternatives it was his duty to follow, if he laid the matter before God in prayer his previous thinking would not be irrelevant, probably, to the final decision. Into his mind composed in prayer would come the arguments he had marshalled, religious teaching that might be relevant, the attitudes and advice of friends he trusted, memories from his subconscious, etc. If clarification and his final decision came merely as a result of this combination of factors no divine activity would be involved. There would be no "answer to prayer." The final decision would depend simply on that clarification of the mind that is the result of quiet meditation. However, if in addition to all the ideas in his mind the power of God's Holy Spirit assisted him directly in sorting out his ideas, and to a slight extent weighted his decision, then you have a genuine answer to prayer and a breaking of the creation barrier. For at some point the man's mind would have taken on the influence of an extra-natural Spirit and at that point the neurological

---

[1] Matthew 6:11.
[2] Mark 14:36.

activity that accompanies thought would take on a corresponding slight modification which would be the result of no cause within the natural order but would have a strictly supernatural cause. And so at that particular juncture there would be a break in the regular cause and effect sequences of the natural order, as they are seen by science from within the natural order.

The same thing can be shown to hold true if one considers the prayer for personal peace of mind. If a man lying awake nights worrying himself into nervous indigestion prays for spiritual peace and receives it, the rhythm of his bodily functions will become serene and even. If the attainment of the peace that he prayed for was due entirely to auto-suggestion no breaking of the creation barrier and no answer to prayer is involved. The man had inappropriately prayed for something that could only be obtained by auto-suggestion, but his prayer had unintentionally functioned as auto-suggestion and so he had received the appropriate benefit. If, however, when the man prayed, the power of God had actually impinged upon his spirit to initiate the experience of peace, then at that point his neural activity which governed the functioning of his bodily organs would be receiving an effect for which there was no natural cause. In other words there would be at that point a breaking of the creation barrier.

Niebuhr does not admit that God ever breaks the creation barrier in response to men's prayers. Niebuhr posits no divine action at all even in response to the prayer for strength of the dying martyr. He says that in the instance of the dying martyr the strength with "which the ordinary resources of nature are supplemented"[1] is due to the "pressures of a given moment which endow the individual with resources beyond his natural capacities."[2] "The crisis with its impending martyrdom adds its emotional pressures to

---

[1] ICE. p. 215de.
[2] ICE. p. 216d.

81

the commitment of previous years. Furthermore, a strong devotion to a cause absorbs the individual in the cause so that the entire socio-spiritual impetus of the enterprise sustains him in the hour of crisis and endows him with resources which transcend anything possessed in his own right."[1]

Not only does the martyr's strength come to him entirely from within the creation but there is also no glad assurance in Niebuhr's theology that after the close of his martyrdom God will break the creation barrier and take his faithful servant to a joyous life in heaven with himself. The martyr would only have the satisfaction and recompense in the moments before his death in the knowledge that what he did and what he stood for "is ultimately right and true."[2] Niebuhr admits that this is a "tragic conception" and asks, "Is history a constant repetition of the triumph of evil on the plane of the obvious and is the triumph of the good merely the inner triumph of its own assurance of being right?"[3] His books nowhere contain a reasoned optimistic answer to this question. He does not feel, however, that God is proved unjust if death ends everything for a man, because "logically every life deserves destruction. Since it is predatory either individually or collectively, it ought to die at the hands of those it has exploited."[4] Niebuhr quotes with approval Marcus Aurelius' saying that everything happens " 'either in such a wise as thou art formed by nature to bear it or . . . as thou art not formed by nature to bear it

---

[1] ICE. p. 217ab. In Niebuhr's later books he does not take a stand that contradicts this statement as can be seen from the next quotation from *Human Destiny*. For this reason I have stressed this passage on martyrdom from Niebuhr's early book *An Interpretation of Christian Ethics*, even though Niebuhr said later, "I was only dimly feeling my way in this book toward a realistic and valid Christian ethic. I disavowed some of my ideas and amended others in later works, which roughly represent my present position." Quoted from Charles W. Kegley and Robert W. Bretall, Editors, *Reinhold Niebuhr His Religious, Social, and Political Thought* (New York: The Macmillan Company, 1956), pp. 434, 435.

[2] (2)HD. p. 45ef; SNE. p. 134d; SNE. p. 298ab.

[3] (2)HD. p. 45f, 46a.

[4] REE. p. 285e.

.... But if it happens in such wise as thou art not formed by nature to bear it, do not complain because it will perish after it has consumed thee!' "[1] Niebuhr comments that "the advice may be regarded as a wholesome reminder of human creatureliness. Indeed Stoic wisdom is a good antidote to man's whining inclination to deny the fact of his mortality."[2]

A God as passive in the face of human need as the picture of God which emerges from Niebuhr's description seems cold and loveless. This is why Niebuhr can never talk about God's relation to individual men and why Niebuhr's theology offers little day by day help to a person struggling to be a Christian amid the difficulties of life. It explains also why Niebuhr is much more at ease when he is talking about God's relationship to man in the mass, to collective man.

But if God is cold and loveless in his relation to individual men is he a loving God? For by definition love seeks communion with the beloved and takes practical steps for the beloved's welfare. Furthermore, love is basically the love of one spiritual being for another spiritual being. Love is not basically felt toward mass man, collective man. If we ask *how* God is shown to live up to this definition of love we shall see that we draw a blank in Niebuhr's theology. But love according to Niebuhr is the crown and completion of morality.[3] Without the emphasis on morality including of necessity love in order to be morality, much of Niebuhr's polemic against "the nice people," the "pillars of society," loses its force. For the subtle analysis of sin loses its force if sin is not seen as disloyalty to a God who loves one. Niebuhr claims that if philosophy and religion cannot be reconciled it is better to leave some loose ends philosophically rather than have a religion with an inadequate ethic.[4] But following his thought from the point of view of ethical consistency it

---

[1] FH. p. 63cd.
[2] FH. p. 63d.
[3] (2) HD. p. 56e.
[4] DCNR. p. 214b-d.

is seen that his refusal to admit that God can and does break the creation barrier undermines his ethics.

In religion man craves to be related to God. It is Niebuhr's claim that the "self is related to God in repentance, faith, and commitment. All these forms of relation imply a certain degree of existential discontinuity with God. The self is always a creature, conscious of its finiteness, and equally conscious of its pretension in not admitting its finiteness."[1] But this typical quotation of Niebuhr's is seen, upon analysis, to omit all mention of activity upon God's part. For man's repentence, faith, and commitment are the description of only the human side of the relation to God. So by themselves they are an insufficient description because in a relationship there must be activity on the part of both parties to the relationship. *What Niebuhr should have said and did not say is that man's repentance, faith, and commitment are his role in the relationship and that to a man in the state of repentence, faith, and commitment God relates himself favorably.* Niebuhr cannot say this because Niebuhr's God never relates himself to any individual. Since man cannot crash heaven, in a relationship to man God would have to come to man; and since man is a part of nature this would involve breaking the creation barrier. The idea expressed in the words "my Father will love him, and we will come to him and make our home with him,"[2] taken to refer to the coming of the Holy Spirit,[3] is entirely foreign to Niebuhr.

Paul Lehman in his article "The Christology of Reinhold Niebuhr" says that the relation of the Holy Spirit to Christ, and "the power by which this wisdom and power effectively works" is almost undealt with in Niebuhr's theology.[4] And Hans Hofmann in *The Theology of Reinhold*

---

[1] SDH. pp. 84f, 85a.
[2] John 14:23.
[3] John 16:12-15.
[4] Charles W. Kegley and Robert W. Bretall, editors, *Reinhold Niebuhr His Religious, Social, and Political Thought* (New York: The Macmillan Company, 1956), pp. 277,278.

Niebuhr questions in his conclusion whether Niebuhr's theology does not "require a much fuller interpretation of the doctrine of the Holy Spirit?" Dr. Hofmann continues:

> The Holy Spirit is God's complete personal turning to each one of us in order to promise him personally redemption through Christ and to create in him the work of 'becoming new.' Niebuhr, who pondered so earnestly the meaning of God, the Father and the Son, seems to have found a difficulty in the person of the Holy Spirit.[1]

Gordon Harland voices the same opinion:

> It must be acknowledged that discerning and sympathetic critics seem to agree that the most obvious and serious defect in Niebuhr's apologetic lies right at this point, in an inadequate understanding of the Church or, what is intimately related, in his defective doctrine of the Holy Spirit. . . . Paul Scherer also regrets that the doctrines of the Holy Spirit and the Church receive 'little attention' in Niebuhr's sermons.[2]

It is odd that Dr. Lehman and Dr. Hofmann and Dr. Harland should appear to think accidental the omission of any adequate treatment of the doctrine of the Holy Spirit. For in Christian thought the Holy Spirit is Deity himself at work in the hearts of Christians. But the claim that the Holy Spirit works in the hearts of Christians involves the claim that within their lives the creation barrier is constantly broken by the supernatural Being of Deity within the human being (who as human is part of nature) helping the human individual and gradually modifying his life by the Power that is beyond nature. In other words, regenera-

---

[1] Hans Hofmann, *The Theology of Reinhold Niebuhr* (New York: Charles Scribner's Sons, 1956), p. 246.

[2] Gordon Harland, *The Thought of Reinhold Niebuhr* (New York: Oxford University Press, 1960), p. 150.

tion and sanctification by the Holy Spirit involve miracle, and miracle is steadily denied in Niebuhr's teaching.

The question of whether the Holy Spirit is actually at work in the world—and therefore a breaking of the creation barrier is taking place—is the Christian form of the problem of how revelation took place as regards the Biblical prophets in Old Testament times. Niebuhr has claimed that Christianity is a religion of revelation, that this distinguishes it from the pagan religions which are man made. In the Old Testament times if the direct and immediate action of God helped form the ideas in a prophet's mind, a breaking of the creation barrier, i.e., miracle, took place. The giving of the Law at Sinai and the experience of St. Paul on the road to Damascus are cases in point.

We know that even before Moses went up on Mt. Sinai he was holding court among the people and describing his decisions to Jethro as making the people "know the statutes of God and his decisions."[1] Moses already had in his humanly acquired experience a knowledge of Egyptian laws and administrative ways, a knowledge of the lore of his own people with its origin in the south and north Euphrates valley (regions famous for their great law codes), and a knowledge of the needs and customs of desert life acquired in his exile years in Midian with Jethro. If the amalgam of this knowledge in his brilliant mind was all that is involved in the giving of the Law at Sinai, then Moses' forty days on the mountain can be fully described as the father of his people getting away from the children for a time for a little peace and quiet to *think things through*. If, however, on the mountain this human thinking was assisted and guided by God in the assembling of the laws, and if God illumined Moses' understanding as to the significance of moral law in relating man to God, then there was real revelation— and a breaking of the creation barrier. For at some points in Moses' thinking the physio-neural brain activity that ac-

---

[1] Exodus 18:16.

companied his thinking would have undergone a slight modification for which there was no physical cause. That the amount of matter involved would have been infinitesimally small does not alter the fact that Deity would have broken the creation barrier at those particular points by using his direct influence to effect some modification in the natural order.

The same problem presents itself in Paul's vision on the Damascus road. If all that was involved was an emotional upheaval from the subconscious, reversing his estimate of Stephen's death and bringing to a close the personal struggle of Paul's own long years of spiritual uneasiness, then no special contact with a literally risen Christ took place, and no revelation and no breaking of the creation barrier was involved. And the voice that he heard and the light that he saw were hallucinations due entirely to the intensity of his emotional experience. If however Christ who is Deity, having Paul's memory of the death of Stephen and Paul's emotional nature and long history of emotional uneasiness as raw material upon which to work, actually on the road to Damascus put a pressure to bear upon Paul which was the deciding factor in finally convincing him that Jesus is Lord, then at that point you have a real revelation and a breaking of the creation barrier. For at some point the physio-neural activity that accompanied the conscious thinking of Paul would have undergone a slight modification for which there was no cause that was part of our universe. That the amount of matter involved would have been infinitesimally slight does not alter the fact that a breaking of the creation barrier would have taken place.

So embarrassing is the belief in a genuine breaking of the creation barrier, that modern theologians who have felt the need to turn from modern philosophical substitutes for religion to the religion of the Bible, which is a religion of revelation, have been hard put to it to make a convincing description of revelation and still deny that God breaks the creation barrier. They attempt to claim a non-miraculous form of revelation (1) by denying that the content of Old Testament revelation was specific messages or instructions, (2) by insisting that the content of relevation is the self-unveiling of the character of God, and (3) by describing the *modus operandi* of revelation as the "intercourse of mind and event which is the essence of revelation."[1] Reinhold Niebuhr's idea of revelation is in line with this.

In trying to estimate the adequacy of such an interpretation of revelation it is well to point out that it does not accept what is obvious to anyone who reads the Bible carefully, namely that the Bible claims that God does give messages with a specific content to the prophets, and that some of the messages are messages to private situations rather than statements of universal truths. There are innumerable instances of this. The definition of the role of the prophet in the burning bush incident where God says "He (Aaron) shall be a mouth for you (Moses), and you shall be to him as God"[2] is a case in point. So also in the story of the call of Samuel the message of doom to the house of Eli was a specific message,[3] although it stressed what Israel considered God's permanent distaste for graft. The revelation of God to Nathan that David should not build a temple at Jerusalem and that God would establish David's dynasty forever is also specific.[4] The message of God to Elijah at Horeb in which he is told to anoint two men as future kings and to select Elisha to be his own prophetic successor is certainly not a universal truth applicable to all men.[5] Neither is God's command to Hosea to take "a wife of harlotry and have children of harlotry,"[6] or God's promise to Hezekiah through Isaiah that Sennacherib would hear a rumor and

---

[1] John Baillie, *The Idea of Revelation in Recent Thought* (New York: Columbia University Press, 1956), p. 110.

[2] Exodus 4:16.

[3] I Samuel 3:13,14.

[4] IISamuel 7:4-17.

[5] I Kings 19:15-17.

[6] Hosea 1:2.

return to his own land without taking Jerusalem unspecific.[1]
God's initial call to the young Jeremiah is personal:

> Before I formed you in the womb I knew you, and
> before you were born I consecrated you; I appointed
> you a prophet to the nations.[2]

And in his later years his "word of the Lord" in his letter
giving practical advice to the exiles in Babylonia is distinctly
specific.[3]

It is easy to caricature the Old Testament idea of prophecy by describing it as a kind of divine dictation to the
prophet, and then to discredit Old Testament prophetic
claims by discrediting the caricature. The prophets were
certainly not primarily clairvoyants foretelling the future.
As God's will is stable, the revealing of his will is the deline-
ation of his character, and so modern theologians are partly
right when they claim that prophecy is the self-unveiling of
God. And yet they are not wholly right, for the phrase "the
self-unveiling of God" conjures up in the mind of the
reader a static picture of a Divine that can be more and
more fully contemplated, as in the Platonic sense one can
contemplate more and more completely the good, the beautiful, and the true. The Hebrew God is always thought of as
active, with specific immediate and long distance purposes
he wishes to carry out. Man is therefore thought of not as
the contemplator of God but as the servant of God. When
man comes into intimate contact with God it is to receive
directions for the next job at hand. This fact makes it impossible for a Christian who remains true to Biblical religion
to by-pass the embarrassment of the problem of revelation
by trying to reduce its entire content to God's "self-unveiling" and by denying completely that specific messages are
ever transmitted directly from God to a man. When St. Paul

---

[1] II Kings 19:6,7.
[2] Jeremiah 1:5.
[3] Jeremiah 29:1-14.

89

was describing his conversation to King Agrippa he concluded by saying, "Wherefore, O King Agrippa, I was not disobedient to the heavenly vision."[1] Dr. J. S. Whale comments: "Only a Hebrew would talk of obeying a vision."[2] A Greek would not have obeyed a vision, he would have contemplated it. Because man is God's servant given by him tasks to perform for God, the Biblical idea of revelation regularly contains a future reference, although it is true that the sum total of the specific instances of revelation is a self-unveiling of the character of God, as the total of an earthly executive's orders are a self-unveiling of the man's character. But if a great human executive says to his secretary, "Ask Mr. Jones to take the visiting client out to lunch," that specific instruction, in the sense of having reference to future action, in some sense foretells the future. Thus, although Hebrew prophets were primarily engaged in showing God's character and will to the people, nevertheless, because God's will is an active will, reference to the future is an integral part of Hebrew prophecy.

Although the Old Testament would frown on a claim that any man was "pally with the Deity,"[3] real social intercourse between the prophet and God is implied. One can hold this without having to hold a theory of divine dictation and without holding that all the passages prefixed with the formula "thus saith the Lord" are the *ipsissima verba* of Deity. There were many prophets who said, "Thus saith the Lord," who were not finally acknowledged as important spokesmen of God and whose sayings are not recorded in the Bible. Our Old Testament is the distillation of the record of the religious experience of Israel as the consensus of opinion of lesser devout men chose for permanent treasuring those religious records through which God's character,

---

[1] Acts 26:19.

[2] J. S. Whale, *Christian Doctrine* (New York: The Macmillan Co., 1941), p. 55.

[3] A phrase of Dr. Farmer's quoted by J. S. Whale in his *Christian Doctrine* (New York: The Macmillan Co., 1941), p. 57.

will, and activity could be most clearly seen in generations of testing by the ongoing religious life of Israel. The distinction between prophet and either priest or rabbi in Hebrew thought is that the priest and rabbi learned from human sources the cultus or teaching which they transmitted, while there was that in the prophet's message that was due to the direct teaching of God. We can see that the prophet could have learned his message by means of direct contact with God while at the same time the prophetic messages may not be the *ipsissima verba* of God, if we compare the learning process of the prophet in the presence of God with the learning process of a teen-age student obtaining spiritual or cultural insight in the society of a human teacher. Neither the divine nor the human teacher works with a mind that is a *tabula rasa*.

Often we forget that the method by which the pupil learns from the human teacher is almost as much of a mystery as the way the human being learns from God. Veteran teachers have the experience of former pupils telling them fifteen or twenty years later that something they said or did made a lasting and guiding impression upon their lives, and the teacher does not really know how the important teaching was effected. The pupil comes to the human teacher with a mind already furnished with a store of personal experience, with a good deal of secondhand experience from previous schooling, and with more or less special personal interests and problems. The teacher teaches by moving around in the pupils' minds information that they already possess, for vocabulary is itself a kind of information, and so are the larger concepts where a brief phrase will serve to raise in the mind a whole constellation of ideas. (If a teacher who spoke Japanese were to try to teach American students, no teaching would result, because the students would not already know Japanese, and so the teacher would not be moving about in the pupils' minds ideas with which their minds were already furnished.) Each pupil tries to amalgamate the ideas the teacher is bringing into focus in his mind with that part of the furnishing of his mind that he already has in focus. The pupils usually do not understand fully the implications of what the teacher is saying, and the previous experience of each individual furnishes in the case of each pupil a different set of ideas to amalgamate with those the teacher is bringing into focus, and sometimes the most peculiar accounts drift back to the teacher of the way his sayings have been repeated. Nevertheless when all allowances have been made it is really true that some of the teacher's insight does get across to the pupils and their younger minds do develop in knowledge and spiritual maturity partly by contact with the mature living mind of the teacher.

Any veteran teacher of English literature or religion who loves to teach is aware as the years pass that a considerable amount of learning has taken place in his general vicinity without his really understanding how it has happened. He never really knows how it is that when he rearranges ideas already in a student's mind new ideas emerge, or old ideas take on increasing significance. Also any experienced teacher knows that a pupil learns not at the point at which the pupil hears the sound of the teacher's words but at the point at which the idea conveyed by the words registers upon the pupil's mind, which is a very different matter, alas! Certainly no one with experience in teaching should worry about how God could convey a particular message to a prophet without using words that could be heard by the ear of the prophet. When God speaks to a prophet he can by-pass the speaking-hearing apparatus, and begin his teaching at the point at which he registers an idea upon his pupil's mind.

The point at which the pupil spiritually hears the human teacher and the point at which the prophet hears the Divine Teacher are both in the learner's mind. The human teacher must make use of the speaking-hearing apparatus in order to contact the pupil's mind. God who is spirit and the creator of the human mind can contact it directly without recourse to the speaking-hearing apparatus. What the prophet is aware of is that ideas are being rearranged in his mind. As prophets are aware of what transpires in their minds they know that they themselves sometimes rearrange ideas, that is, they think. Sometimes they experience a rearranging that they do not initiate, which seems to be done to them and which they consider the impact of God upon their lives.

One cannot prove by exterior arguments whether this arranging of ideas that seems to be done to them is ever direct Divine teaching or always merely the upsurge of ideas from the subconscious. We only know that those who knew best what was in the prophets' minds, namely the prophets themselves, believed that direct Divine assistance was included in their messages beyond the ability of their merely human thinking and their minds' reservoir of half forgotten past experiences. If there is any direct Divine assistance in the rearranging of the ideas in the prophet's mind, there the creation barrier has been broken. This theory of the Divine method of teaching would apply to the guidance of the lives of ordinary Christians by the Holy Spirit, not just to a handful of great prophets in ancient Israel. For this reason it is probably inadequate as a complete account of prophetic inspiration. It is presented here as a minimum theory of the method of divine revelation that will allow for real intercourse of the Supernatural Spirit of the Creator and the natural spirit of a man the creature. If the Spirit of God did no more than assist in concentrating the human being's interest upon certain ideas already in his mind rather than on others, and of making a *yes* or *no* response to alternatives the human mind presented to God in prayer, the miraculous breaking of the creation barrier would still be involved.

It is a mistake to think that the twentieth century is the first century to be critical on the subject of divine inspiration. The Middle Ages, which did not question the possibility of the intercourse of the Supernatural with men, and which cultivated by prayer, fasting, and expectation the ability to have visionary experience, had to sort out what could be thought of as genuine Divine teaching from a superabundance of visionary instances, and to identify vision as distinct from mere hallucination. It is interesting to note that visions without audio-visual accompaniments were thought of as having the greatest depth and validity. And the test of whether a vision had a divine origin was whether its long distance effect was to purify, strengthen, clarify, and bring inner peace and greater devotion to God to the person who had experienced it. If the vision did not have these long distance effects it could be written off as merely emotional excitement of some kind or the work of the devil masquerading as an angel of light.[1]

The same problem was dealt with from another angle by George Fox, the founder of Quakerism. He made the government of the Quakers dependent upon the direct guidance of the Holy Spirit, which he called the Light Within, and then he was forced to find a way in which anything as personal and unpredictable as divine guidance could serve for group administration. He defined the Divine Light "which lighteth every man that cometh into the world"[2] as "the light which shows a man evil" and as "the light in which is unity."[3] That is, the Divine could be depended upon to constantly fence off the evil alternative from those lives that were religiously devout, and to foster the mystical unity with God and with one another of those who were religiously devout. This is the unspectacular but steady working of God in human life that can be tested by generations of those living the religious life.

All this points in the same direction. All people have the experience at the merely human level of having their spirits grow in the presence of someone maturer than them-

---

[1] Evelyn Underhill, *Mysticism A Study in the Nature and Development of Man's Spiritual Consciousness* (New York: E. P. Dutton and Company, 1911), pp. 323, 327-330, 334-336.

[2] King James Version, John 1:9.

[3] See Rachel H. King, *George Fox and the Light Within, 1650-1660* (Philadelphia: Friends Book Store, 1940).

94

selves. It is by the experience of spiritual growth in the prayer life that the devout have recognized that they were being educated by the Divine Teacher.

The hypothetical description of revelation as including the direct activity of God refocusing ideas in the prophet's mind to teach him, as the human teacher refocuses ideas already in the pupil's mind in the process of teaching and training him to greater maturity, would seem to me the minimum interpretation that could be given if one is to interpret the incidents of Moses receiving the Law at Sinai and Paul being converted on the road to Damascus as involving real intercourse of Deity with the human mind. And if intercourse with the Supernatural (i.e., Deity) and the human mind takes place at all there the creation barrier is broken. *If such intercourse does not take place the revelation of the Law to Moses on Mt. Sinai means only that on Mt. Sinai Moses thought things through, and the conversion of Paul on the road to Damascus would be fully explained as an eruption of suppressed ideas from his subconscious.* If these were the full explanations, God would have to be described in Pantheistic or at best Deistic terms. He would not be the God of the Bible.

We have mentioned before that modern theology in discussing revelation has tended to say that revelation is God's self unveiling, and that the method of revelation lies in the interaction of mind with event. Let us now investigate this idea more fully as we turn to Reinhold Niebuhr's theory of revelation.

In line with some of the outstanding modern European theologians Niebuhr claims that God reveals himself in his mighty acts in history.[1] According to this theory God took Israel out of slavery in Egypt and saved them at the Red Sea and established his Covenant with them at Sinai,[2] and

---

[1] (1) HN. p. 136ef; FH. p. 22cd.
[2] FH. p. 24cd.

the prophetic mind meditating upon these events saw in them a revelation of the character of God.[1] But we must know what we mean when we say that God took Israel out of slavery and saved them at the Red Sea. It does not mean for modern theologians including Niebuhr that God broke through the creation barrier to give them miraculous assistance. It merely means that Moses had thought things through at an incident of a burning bush (often by Liberal critics interpreted as a bush aflame with the colors of autumn foliage) and had decided that the time was ripe and that it was his duty to lead Israel out of Egypt. And then a constellation of entirely naturally caused events, the plagues, so occupied the Egyptians' minds that the time was propitious for Israel to make a get-away from Egypt under Moses' leadership. And further, that the fortunate occurrence, entirely naturally caused, of a strong east wind lowering the level of the Red Sea to a fordable depth at the exact time when Israel approached it, saved them at the frontier from being encircled by a pincers movement of Pharaoh's overtaking chariots. So far God's "mighty acts" are simply fortunate coincidences in nature, events that in the natural course of events would have occurred even if Israel had not been enslaved in Egypt.

Well and good, but we must also ask ourselves, did the prophets entirely on their own make the connection between the fortunately coincidental natural events of the Exodus and their interpretation of it as God's saving "mighty act"? If the connection between the Exodus and their interpretation of it was made entirely on their own, then all that can be said is that the Hebrew race produced some individuals who were particularly skillful at constructing a picture of the character of God from particular events which they themselves selected from all the possible events of which they had knowledge. In that case it would be more accurate to say that they deduced the person and character of God

---

[1] FH. pp. 24f-25a.

from their arbitrarily self-chosen incidents than it would be to say that God revealed himself to them. For all the initiative that made the difference between "revelation" and "no revelation" lay wholly on their side. Why they should be able to find God's character revealed in these particular events rather than in some other different type of events remains a mystery.[1] And there is no explanation of why it should have been Hebrew minds rather than Chinese minds that over the centuries made religiously appropriate inter-relations of mind with event.

If one says that the Hebrew people saw God's character in this and in other particular events because God focused their minds on these particular events as being particularly revelatory, then God at these points broke the creation barrier to so focus their minds. For if the merely human activity of human minds with their concomitant neural activity were insufficient to produce the appropriate focusing and concentration, then at that point there was the miracle of the breaking of the creation barrier; for at that point there would be, concomitant to their conscious minds, a physio-neural activity initiated for which there was no cause that was itself the effect from a previous cause *within* the creation. That the physical modification here involved was infinitesimally slight does not alter the fact that miracle would have occurred.

Incidentally if God steered or concentrated the minds of the Hebrew people in this way there would be an adequate explanation of why it was the Hebrews and not the Chinese who made "that intercourse of mind and event which is the essence of revelation." God would have *chosen* to steer the Hebrew minds and not the Chinese minds. Or if one is perturbed at the thought of God showing partiality to a particular people one can say that he chose Israel because this particular people were most amenable to this divine steering and focusing of the mind. One can allow for an

---

[1] FH. pp. 105f-106acd.

immense amount of native spiritual insight and initiative on the part of Israel. But if that totally accounts for the prophetic movement then Hebrew religion is a man made affair and not a religion of revelation. If, however, the native Hebrew spiritual initiative and insight were at all reinforced by the direct action of God steering their thinking and focusing their attention upon particular events then real revelation—and genuine miracle—would have taken place.

Niebuhr tries to deal with the difficulties in this area of thought by saying that there are two types of revelation, general and special. The special revelations are the mighty historical acts of God such as saving Israel at the Red Sea. These acts, it will be remembered, are being thought of as entirely naturally caused events with no breaking of the creation barrier involved. The general revelation is the fact that men find, when they push their consciousness to its limits, that merely human consciousness is inadequate and that there is something beyond. It is this general revelation interacting with an acquaintance at first or second hand with the special revelatory events, says Niebuhr, that produces what we call revelation in the Old Testament. His key descriptive statement about revelation is in Volume I of *The Nature and Destiny of Man*:

> The revelation of God to man is always a two-fold one, a personal individual revelation, and a revelation in the context of social-historical experience. Without the public and historical revelation the private experience of God would remain poorly defined and subject to caprice. Without the private revelation of God, the public and historical revelation would not gain credence. Since all men have, in some fashion, the experience of a reality beyond themselves, they are able to entertain the more precise revelations of the character and purpose of God as they come to them in the most significant experiences of prophetic history. Private revelation is, in a sense, synonymous with 'general'

revelation, without the presuppositions of which there could be no 'special' revelation. It is no less universal for being private. Private revelation is the testimony in the consciousness of every person that his life touches a reality beyond himself, a reality deeper and higher than the system of nature in which he stands. . . . The experience of God is not so much a separate experience, as an overtone implied in all experience.[1]

Since all the people in Israel had the individual general revelation, and since all had experienced or heard of the revelatory historical events, this theory has no explanation to give of why it was that only a very few Israelites were prophets. Since all the people were experiencers of both kinds of revelation it should have followed that all were prophets, if Niebuhr's explanation of prophecy is correct. And for that matter all twentieth century American Bible students have as much "general revelation" as Isaiah and Jeremiah had. We have also as much "special revelation" as those two prophets had, for we like them can learn from writings now in our Old Testament the account of God's "mighty acts" at the time of the Exodus.[2] Niebuhr's theory therefore gives no explanation of why all earnest twentieth century Americans who are well acquainted with the accounts in the Old Testament are not prophets.

In private or individual "general revelation" the Deity does not *touch* the human individual. God is here described as completely inactive. It is the human person whose life, according to Niebuhr, "touches a reality beyond himself." Furthermore, this human experience is common to all men. We are therefore not given a reason of why the Hebrew nation included prophets and why the Eskimos, the Romans, and the Chinese did not include among their number a series of prophets whose minds had the appropriate intercourse

---

[1] (1) HN. p. 127b-e.
[2] Both Isaiah and Jeremiah could have had access to the J and E documents.

with certain natural events in history which their minds selected as revelatory.

It is also to be noted that, according to this quotation, the experience of God common to all people is an undifferentiated experience. In this central quotation on Niebuhr's theory of revelation no specific moral or aesthetic content is ascribed to the experience of general revelation. It looks as if all that Niebuhr is saying is that men are numinously aware that a Deeper Something exists beyond themselves and the world of sense experience. Niebuhr says that "the experience of God is not so much a separate experience, as an overtone implied in all experience." If this means literally what it says then the divine overtone in life would be experienced indiscriminately in such widely differing experiences as swimming, carrying a Thanksgiving basket to the poor, taking out life insurance, tying one's shoe laces, listening to a symphony, committing adultery with one's neighbor's wife, hailing a bus, paying one's income tax, cheating at solitaire, attending a Rotary Club meeting, getting drunk, going to church, doing research on cancer, committing murder, etc. Any experience that was an undifferentiated overtone to all these experiences would be as completely nonmoral and non-intellectual as the state of one's digestion. Niebuhr admits that "a general revelation can only point to the reality of God but not to His particular attributes. A theology which believes only in a general revelation must inevitably culminate in pantheism."[1] Niebuhr's belief that God is personal could therefore not be derived from general revelation. The sense of touching at all points of life a reality deeper and higher than the obvious system of nature in which one stands is the background for the Hindu search for Deity, that seeks safety in the Oneness of the All-Embracing at the expense of jettisoning the importance of ethical distinctions. The words "deeper" and "higher" that Niebuhr uses for this reality are not in themselves moral

---

[1] BT. p. 15de.

words. Since we sometimes use these spacial words meta-phorically to indicate moral degree, his use of them here in regard to revelation conveys the impression of his having said that in their inmost souls all men personally meet God making ethical demands—which in the nature of the case have to be specific—upon them. Such a claim if specifically made would describe God as personally interacting with the consciences of men and admit a belief in the possibility of breaking the creation barrier. This Dr. Niebuhr is very care-ful not to do in these passages. But if one is reading rapidly without paying much attention to this particular problem one tends to get the impression that he has made the admis-sion of specific divine intercourse with the human soul, or that he soon will make it. It is only when one searches his writings carefully that one realizes that the admission is not actually made.

This is in line with what I said earlier, namely that Niebuhr is forced into a kind of revived Deist position in his attempt to keep his description of God moral and Bibli-cal and at the same time never to question science's assump-tion that nature's cause and effect sequences are unbroken. My contention is that Niebuhr is searching desperately for some middle ground that will allow him to keep Biblical Christianity while denying that the supernatural God ever interferes directly in the affairs of men, and that Niebuhr fails, because this denial eventually undercuts his claim that God is righteously loving. This makes a basic inner incon-sistency in Niebuhr's whole pattern of thought, because he is attempting to restate Christianity following the require-ments of ethical logic. In the interests of ethical consistency he has been willing to leave philosophical consistency at somewhat loose ends.[1] But he hesitates to follow his ethical logic to its full conclusion. For he undermines his claim that God is righteously loving by refusing to admit God's break-

---

[1] DCNR. p. 214b-d.

ing the creation barrier, and so he ends up without ethical consistency.

It is hard to claim against Niebuhr and against the trend of twentieth century American Christianity in general that the supernatural God can and does interfere in the affairs of men, and to claim that belief in this interference is essential to Christian theology. When one does insist on this, educated people have a way of simply assuming that one is intellectually old fashioned and naive and that one has not outgrown an infantile Santa Claus conception of God. So I shall try to make very clear what I mean by God's interfering in the affairs of men by comparing Niebuhr's just discussed account of "general" and "special" revelation with St. Augustine's description of his first clear cut experience of the presence of God. Niebuhr has claimed that "general" or "private" revelation "is the testimony in the consciousness of every person that his life touches a reality beyond himself, a reality deeper and higher than the system of nature in which he stands. . . . The experience of God is not so much a separate experience, as an overtone implied in all experience."[1]

By comparison Augustine says:

(A) I entered into my inward self, *Thou leading me on;* and I was able to do it, for *Thou wert become my helper.* (B) And I entered, and with the eye of my soul (such as it was) saw above the same eye of my soul, above my mind, the Unchangeable Light. Not this common light, which all flesh may look upon, nor, as it were, a greater one of the same kind . . . but different, very different from all these. (C) *Nor was it above my mind as oil is above water, nor as heaven above earth; but above it was, because it made me, and I below it, because I was made by it.* (D) He who

---

[1] (1) HN. p. 127d.

knows the Truth knows that Light; and he that knows it knoweth eternity. Love knoweth it. O Eternal Truth, *and true Love,* and loved Eternity! Thou art my God. . . . (E) *Thou liftedst me up. . . . Thou didst beat back the infirmity of my sight, pouring forth upon me most strongly Thy beams of light, and* I trembled with love and fear; (F) *and I found myself to be far off from Thee, in the region of dissimilarity,* (G) *as if* I heard this voice of Thine from on high: 'I am the food of strong men; grow, and thou shalt feed upon me.' . . . (H) *And Thou criedst to me from afar, 'Yea, verily, I AM THAT I AM.'* And I heard this, as things are heard in the heart, nor was there room for doubt; (I) and I should more readily doubt that I live than that Truth is not, which is clearly seen, *being understood by the things that are made.*[1]

According to this description of Augustine's, God is supernatural to the creation but not spacially supernatural (C) (F) (G). The vision was not audio-visual (B) (G): what he saw was above his mind, and it was only "as if" he heard the voice. And yet the vision is an inter-personal relationship, with Augustine loving and contemplating God and God strengthening, guiding, and illumining Augustine. The verbs relating to God are active verbs: (A) God *led* and *helped* Augustine. (E) God *lifted* him up, *beat back* the infirmity of his sight, and *poured forth* upon him his beams of light, and (G) (H) his *voice cried* to Augustine. In other words, genuine special intercourse between the Creator and a particular creature is taking place and this involves miracle.

William Temple also insists upon the miraculous genuine traffic between God and the human being in the divine-human inter-personal relationship of the religious life. Temple says:

---

[1] *The Confessions.* Book VII Chapter 10. In Whitney J. Oates, Editor, *The Basic Writings of St. Augustine* (New York: Random House, 1948), Volume I. Italics mine.

God has created us as children of His love, able to understand that love in some degree and to respond to it. In the psycho-physical organism of human personality there is the possibility for a development of the spiritual elements, in response to and communion with the eternal God, which makes these capable of receiving from God the gift of His own immortality. . . . Now the Grace of God is His love made known and active upon and within us; and our response to it is both entirely free and entirely due to the activity of His love towards us. All that we could contribute of our own would be the resistance of our self-will.[1]

It is Reinhold Niebuhr's Deistic inability to admit the genuine miraculous intercourse of God and the human soul that forces him to reduce his conception of grace to the statement: "Essentially the experience of grace in religion is the apprehension of the absolute from the perspective of the relative."[2]

In returning to the account of Augustine's vision of God, if we ask ourselves about the intellectual content of the message that is brought to him we find three intellectual items conveyed to Augustine in the experience: (D) God is *true love,* (H) God is *I Am That I AM,* and (G) God instructs his with the message, " '*I am the food of strong men; grow, and thou shalt feed upon me.*' " When we look closely at these three items it becomes obvious that they were already part of the mental equipment of Augustine and that the vision simply made the ideas available to Augustine in a new way. Augustine had an intellectual acquaintance with Christianity at this time through his own wide reading and from his childhood training, from the life and conversation of his mother, and from the sermons of Ambrose. He knew before the onset of the vision that God defined himself to Moses as "I Am That I Am," and that the whole tenor of

---

[1] William Temple, *Nature, Man and God* (London: Macmillan, 1951), pp. 468de, 470a.

[2] REE. p. 281e. And see also REE. p. 285c-e; and (2)HD. p. 246bc, both of which shy away from an admission of miraculous grace.

the New Testament emphasizes that God is love. And even a slight understanding of the Gospel of John and the sacrament of the Lord's Supper[1] would have acquainted him with the idea that the Christian is supposed to feed spiritually upon God.

In other words, if my interpretation is correct, Augustine's vision bears out my contention that there is real individual teaching of the human being directly by God in prophecy, and visions, and the process of sanctification, and that the form of this teaching is somewhat analogous to the cultural or spiritual teaching of pupils by a human teacher. The human teacher also moves about in pupils' minds ideas with which those minds are already furnished—for our complex vocabulary and the constellations of ideas forming the accepted pattern of a civilization's life are highly intellectual mental equipment. The result of this mutual activity on the part of the pupils and teacher is the increase in the pupils' understanding and maturity. And the pupils' learning from both the human and the divine teacher is colored by the minds and personalities of the pupils and is in neither case necessarily completely infallible.

The most curious thing about Augustine's vision is his statement at its close (I). He says, "I should more readily doubt that I live than that Truth is not, which is clearly seen, *being understood by the things that are made.*" Here he seems to be recognizing that empirical knowledge is an ingredient in the content of religiously inspired knowledge, as we have seen it to be in this particular vision of his.[2] In other words, we have here an interesting comparison to the recent modern understanding of revelation which says that the "Bible is the written witness to that intercourse of mind and event which is the essence of revelation."[3] But

---

[1] The knowledge here would be at second hand. Augustine was not yet baptized.

[2] Compare Romans 1:20.

[3] John Baillie, *The Idea of Revelation in Recent Thought* (New York: Columbia University Press, 1956), p. 110.

this modern interpretation, being afraid because of science to admit miracle, tends to ignore or, as Niebuhr does, directly denies the ingredient of the direct, individually exercised, manipulative power of God upon the human mind in the complex experiences of revelation and spiritual illumination. If one deletes special divine activity from instances of revelation and illumination they cease to be instances of divine revelation and illumination and become instead merely high powered instances of human discovery and construction. This would turn the Jewish-Christian tradition into a man-made religion.

We have already discussed the question of God's special activity in human affairs with regard to the Exodus and the giving of the Law to Moses at Sinai. But further discussion is needed of the third important factor in that great constellation of events that is the cornerstone of Hebrew religion, and that is the part God played in the Covenant at Sinai. Niebuhr heavily emphasizes the Covenant. He says:

> The personal encounter (with God) takes place in the context of a framework of meaning defined by a collective encounter between God and His people. The prophets speak to Israel, and finally to individuals in Israel (particularly in the case of Jeremiah and Ezekiel) on the basis of the assumption that God has a covenant with Israel. This covenant is at once the presupposition and the fruit of prophetic inspiration. The Covenant of God with Israel is an article of faith. It is not altogether clear whether it was Moses or Abraham who was the human agent of the covenant. This indicates either a confusion in the tradition or perhaps the collation of two traditions, perhaps stemming respectively from Palestinian and Egyptian sources. But the confusion does not prevent the gradual consolida-

tion of the idea of *the covenant and its service as the ground upon which prophetic thought proceeds.*[1]

By the covenant being the fruit of prophetic inspiration Niebuhr seems to mean that the prophets inherited the account of the covenant from Hebrew religious history and that as they saw ever more deeply into its significance, the final idea of the covenant came to bulk larger in Hebrew thought because of the significance they had seen in it. Niebuhr's statement that the covenant serves "as the ground upon which prophetic thought proceeds" is of great importance for our interpretation of Niebuhr. He has said that private revelation is men's experience of a reality beyond themselves[2] and we have shown that God is not described as acting in this situation and that the experience has no defined intellectual content. Apparently it is just a *feel* that there is a Divine Power beyond one. The prophets then combine this *feeling* with the mighty acts in history that they think are the acts of the Divine Power and by interpreting the acts in history they arrive at a more and more accurate *description of the basic character of God. The basic "act" of God upon which their prophetic interpretation, i.e., their "prophecy," depends is the Covenant of God with Israel at Sinai. Thus according to Niebuhr the interpretation of this event which they as human beings make, and the conclusions which they as human beings draw from it ARE the prophecy of which the Old Testament is the written record.*

An initial question must be faced: how did Israel know in the first place that God had made a covenant with them at Sinai? The account of Israel at Sinai is J and E material, that is, from the earlier sources, not like D and P which were written after Hebrew thought had for a long time been influenced by prophetic thought. J and E were crystallized into written form in the times of Elijah and Amos

---

[1] SDH. p. 85a-c. Italics, mine.
[2] (1) HN. p. 127b-e.

approximately, thus forming the religious background that undergirded prophetic thought as well as showing traces of early prophetic thought. In the account of Israel at Sinai the situation concerning the mountain is described as including thunder, lightnings, thick cloud, smoke, fire, and earthquake.[1] These items just by themselves are natural occurrences of a frightening and non-reassuring type, and of themselves are not indicative of the idea that God had chosen the Hebrew people because he cared for them and wanted to make a covenant with them. Yet there is every reason to believe that the Hebrew people while they were at Sinai did think that God wanted to make a covenant with them, because the whole nation went through an adoption ceremony in which they were united to God by the sacrificial blood that was thrown on them and on the altar, thus tying God and the nation together.[2]

Israel had to know previous to the blood ceremony that God wished to make a covenant with the nation, because Israel went through the ceremony of adoption in obedience to the belief that this was the will of God. How, then, was it revealed to the nation at Sinai that God wanted to make a covenant with them? Obviously Moses told them so![3] Where did Moses get the information? Either Moses invented the idea and so the basic cornerstone of Hebrew religion is entirely man invented and not a matter of divine revelation, or else there was direct influence of God upon Moses' thinking to convince him that God wanted the Covenant. If the latter is the case God exerted a direct influence upon the ideational content of a man's mind. If the idea of the Covenant was entirely man invented there was no breaking of the creation barrier. But if God did in some way exert a direct influence upon the ideational content of Moses'

---

[1] Exodus 19:16-25.
[2] Exodus 24:3-8.
[3] Exodus 2:7-12; 5:1-3; 5:22-6:1; 15:1-18; 19:2,3 (assuming that verses 4-6 are later interpretation); 19:7-17,20,25; 24:3,7,

mind, then a breaking of the creation barrier took place and miracle is involved in the founding of the Hebrew religion.

There is no by-passing this dilemma by claiming that the original Covenant was with Abraham and that Moses would have heard about it in an entirely human fashion as among the traditions of his people.[1] For this explanation only raises the same question of whether Abraham's covenant with God was an entirely man-invented affair, or whether, to cause the covenant to be established, God exerted a direct influence upon the ideational content of Abraham's mind. If the latter is the case then miracle or the breaking of the creation barrier is involved.

If one claims that the Covenant was initiated in the time of Moses it does no good to claim that what came first was an act, the rescue of Israel at the Red Sea, and that the interaction of Moses' mind with this event was the prophetic thought that initiated the idea of the Covenant. For the records make it perfectly plain that only the confidence that God was specially sponsoring Israel gave Moses and Israel the courage to try to break away from the Egyptian slavery. If this confidence was directly God inspired you have a breaking of the creation barrier and so miracle. If this confidence was not directly God inspired then one has to rewrite the Bible to suit one's theory and make the whole Exodus merely a humanly sponsored, humanly engineered get-away for entirely human purposes that succeeded because by a lucky chance Israel got the breaks. This latter secular interpretation is not Dr. Niebuhr's view of the Exodus and the Covenant. On the other hand Niebuhr never admits a breaking of the creation barrier and so he has no intellectual substantiation for a religious view of the Exodus.

The line of direction for Niebuhr's thought on the subject of the total Christian revelation hinges upon his interpretation of the Covenant. He says:

---

[1] FH. p. 24def; SDH. p. 85c.

The principal of meaning for the history of the children of Israel is given by the idea of God's covenant with Israel. The idea of a covenant between a God who is not owned or chosen by Israel but who chooses Israel contains the germs of a conception of universal history which the prophets explicate.[1]

His covenant with Israel can not be explained except by His inscrutable love: 'Because he loved thy fathers, therefore he chose their seed after them.' (Deuteronomy 4:37) 'The Lord did not choose you because ye were more in number than any people; for ye were the fewest of all people (Deuteronomy 7:7). Israel is warned against the pride of self-sufficiency which forgets the factor of grace in history. The day will come 'when thou hast eaten and art full, and hast built goodly houses . . . and when thy herds and thy flocks multiply' when Israel will be tempted to say 'my power and the might of mine hand hath gotten me this wealth' (Deuteronomy 8:12-17). Such confidence in its power and virtue will be a mark of apostasy.[2]

The idea of God choosing Israel as an act of grace, since Israel had no power or virtue to merit the choice, represents a radical break in the history of culture. It is, in a genuine sense, the beginning of revelation; for here a nation apprehends and is apprehended by the true God and not by a divine creature of its own contrivance. The proof of the genuineness of His majesty and the truth of His divinity is attested by the fact that He confronts the nation and the individual as the limit, and not the extension, of its own power and purpose. He is the enemy and judge of every human pretension which transgresses the limits of human finiteness.

Two ideas, basic to a Biblical interpretation of history, are implicit in this radical conception of the relation of God to historical destiny. One is the idea of a universal history. The other is that history is filled with man's proud and pretentious efforts to defy the

---

[1] FH. p. 36b.
[2] FH. p. 104fg.

divine sovereignty, to establish himself as god by his power or virtue, his wisdom or foresight.[1]

Niebuhr's claim that God's choice of Israel was an act of "grace" must be read with the remembrance that his theory of grace[2] is non-miraculous. "Essentially the experience of grace in religion is the apprehension of the absolute from the perspective of the relative."[3]

Niebuhr's whole theory of revelation depends upon the claim that God chose Israel. But he nowhere admits taking literally any Biblical description of God's choosing Israel. The Biblical claim that "the Lord used to speak to Moses face to face, as a man speaks to his friend"[4] is entirely ruled out in Niebuhr's theory of revelation. His description admits only the ongoing of natural events and the interpretive powers of men's minds plus the diffused feeling without ideational content that there is a "reality[5] deeper and higher than the system of nature in which he stands."[6] On Niebuhr's theory Moses and Israel would have to deduce the idea that God wished to make a covenant with the nation from the assistance afforded them by the naturally caused plagues and the naturally caused lowering of the water depth of the Red Sea as a result of a strong wind.[7] After this wholly human deduction from entirely naturally caused events the Covenant is due entirely to the thought and planning of Moses. No room is allowed for God's direct activity. This neglects to explain the obvious Biblical account that makes Moses' initial willingness to undertake the task of leading Israel out of Egypt entirely dependent on the confidence—which he already had—that God had conveyed to him the idea that God was backing them. If the attempt

---

[1] FH. p. 104a-c.
[2] See *ante,* pp. 73-78.
[3] REE. p. 281e.
[4] Exodus 33:11; and see Numbers 12:6-8 and Deuteronomy 34:10.
[5] Reality is not capitalized.
[6] See *ante,* pp. 98, 99; (1) HN. p. 127b-e.
[7] SDH. p. 66cd.

is made to say that he got the confidence of God's backing solely from the stories of the patriarchs which were part of the tradition of his people, one has the old problem of explaining how it was especially revealed to the patriarchs by God that God had especially chosen and was especially guiding this clan. Niebuhr can rather consistently describe the great prophetic thought from Amos on as deductions based on the mighty revelation involved in the Exodus and the establishment of the Covenant[1] which in the Biblical account (but not in Niebuhr's) includes God's giving of the Law. But to make Hebrew religion a religion of revelation as distinct from a man made religion, Niebuhr would have to explain *how* the ideas about the favorable natural events at the time of the Exodus, and the Law, and the Covenant were *communications from God* and not merely human deductions.

It is significant that for Niebuhr the beginning of revelation is only the Exodus and the Covenant. He does not describe the giving of the Law at Sinai in this great constellation of events. The reason is obvious. *If he included the giving of the Law at Sinai as part of the original revelatory act of God he would be forced to admit that God can directly influence the content of man's thought upon specific occasions, and that would be to admit miracle. This admission would be made even if it were claimed that much of the Pentateuchal legislation is of a later date, and the only laws admitted as part of the original divine revelation were the Ten Commandments in their abbreviated form. Niebuhr's theory of revelation forces him to describe the great revelatory event which took place when Israel was at Sinai as an event which does not include God's giving of the Law to Moses for Israel.*

There is omission of the Law in Niebuhr's most extended discussion of the covenant which is in *Faith and*

---

[1] FH. pp. 24f-25b.

History.[1] Niebuhr's thought ascribes the ethical emphasis of Hebrew prophetism to a deduction from the fact of the covenant itself: Since God freely chose his people at Sinai through no merits of their own they owed him loyalty; and therefore after Sinai their self-centeredness was a disloyalty which is the basic sin of pride which is the sin of the fall of man.[2] "In the history of revelation the counterpart of the sense of moral obligation is the covenant relation between God and His people."[3] It is true that loyalty and disloyalty are ethical concepts. But history is full of instances in which unrighteous leaders for selfish reasons have demanded and received personal loyalty to themselves from followers who were aware of the leader's moral shortcomings. So the feeling of personal and national obligation to God involved in the mere fact of the Covenant is not by itself sufficient to account for the prophets' insistent claim that God himself is thoroughly righteous and steadily demands social righteousness of men.

Niebuhr's religious theory is not of a kind that will substantiate the claim that the Exodus and Sinai were genuine revelations to men in which the supernatural Deity actually broke the creation barrier to instruct and help Israel. And yet Niebuhr's subsequent religious teaching is ungrounded if this breaking of the creation barrier did not take place. For he claims that Christ is the final revelation on the ground that in the Old Testament God is revealed as righteous and loving, and Christ is the perfect, and so final,[4] revelation of the relation of love to righteousness.[5] But if

---

[1] FH. Chap. II, pp. 22cd, 24c-25b, 25ef; Chap. VII, pp. 102d, 103g-104b, 105c, 106c-e; Chap. IX, p. 141cd. See also SDH. pp. 66cd, 78ab, 85af.

[2] FH. p. 106c-e.

[3] (1) HN. pp. 137-138b. Niebuhr does mention the Decalogue in connection with the sojourn at Sinai and the Covenant in one place in SDH. pp. 87c-88c. But here he is discussing modern Judaism in comparison with the New Covenant of Christianity, and in connection with "the religious consciousness of the Jews" speaks of God who "enjoined the precepts of the Decalogue."

[4] See p. 122.

[5] FH. pp. 126, 134-138, 142-145.

all the prophets' teaching about God being righteous and loving is only a further interpretation of the Covenant at Sinai—their human minds interacting with the memory of that revelatory event—and if that original revelatory event does not include the giving of the Moral Law, then there is no foundation for saying that in the Old Testament God is "revealed" as righteous, and therefore there is no Old Testament "revelation" of the relation of God's love to his righteousness for Christ to complete. Furthermore, Niebuhr also claims that man's central sin is his pride,[1] which gets its especial heinousness in that it is rebellion against and disloyalty to a loving God.[2] But the emphasis upon God as loving was first brought into clear focus in prophetic thought by Hosea. And according to Niebuhr, Hosea's "prophetic inspiration" that God is loving would have to be comprised of Hosea's historical knowledge of God's "marriage" to the nation at Sinai,[3] plus Hosea's personal deductions as to the implications of marriage based on his own matrimonial experience. But if the establishment of the covenant "marriage" at Sinai turns out not to have been grounded in a directive communication of the supernatural God with Israel at that time (which would involve breaking the creation barrier), the force of Niebuhr's arguments about the nature of sin and the importance of Christ is undermined. Niebuhr never once admits that in the Old Testament period God broke the creation barrier and communicated with men.

Let us ask ourselves whether Niebuhr assumes that God has given direct help in the post-Biblical period in the form of direct guidance, communication, or assistance.

In *The Self and the Dramas of History* in Part One, Niebuhr explains that the self is constantly holding dia-

---

[1] (1) HN. p. 186de.
[2] (2) HD. pp. 55d-56ae.
[3] Hosea 2:14-20; 11:1,3.

logues with itself, with others, and with God. And he poses the question of whether the dialogue between the self and God is real or imaginary.[1] To try to deal with the question of whether the self is in dialogue with God he defines the statement to mean "that the self distinguishes itself by a yearning for the ultimate."[2] And it is only this very modified form of the assertion implied in the question that he attempts to substantiate.[3] Niebuhr's rephrasing of the proposition to be substantiated from "the self is in dialogue with God" to "the self distinguishes itself by a yearning for the ultimate,"[4] and then his dealing with the proposition only in its revised form eliminates the necessity of claiming that God exhibits any activity relative to the human self. A dialogue involves interaction between two selves and both parties to the dialogue are active. But in the statement, "The self distinguishes itself by a yearning for the ultimate,"[5] only the human self is described as active: it has a yearning. However, as far as the range of that statement goes the "ultimate" is completely inactive.

Niebuhr goes on to say that Judaism and Christianity "interpret the self's experience with the ultimate in the final reaches of its self-awareness as a dialogue with God."[6]

> The encounter of the self with God is defined in Biblical faith in terms of a norm which has been set by an historical 'revelation.' And this revelation is an historical event or series of events which are not essentially miraculous (miracles such as the 'virgin birth' are afterthoughts) but are events in history which are discerned by faith to have revelatory power into the ultimate mystery. Both Biblical religions are covenant faiths, which organize covenant communities upon

---

[1] SDH. p. 1.
[2] SDH. p. 5ac.
[3] SDH. Chapter 12. "The Self and Its Search For Ultimate Meaning."
pp. 61-72.
[4] Ultimate is not capitalized.
[5] SDH. p. 5c.
[6] SDH. p. 64e.

the basis of a common commitment of faith in the divine significance of these events.[1]

Here again in Niebuhr's statement the only claim is that one's direct knowledge of God is as the mystery, the divine greater than man that man is aware of at the outer edge of his own consciousness. But this experience of itself has no ideational content and lacks giving any impression that the Divine is acting in a particular way toward the individual, It is the individual who interprets this undifferentiated experience in terms of particular events in past history.

Under a previous discussion of the self in conversation with other human selves Niebuhr makes this illuminating observation:

> There are no geographic or temporal limits for the self's dialogue with others. Some of the significant dialogues are carried on with the heroes of the past or with a deceased parent or absent lover. The dialogue in such cases may seem to lack the 'other,' so necessary for the dialogue. But memories will furnish the stuff for the dialogue which are almost as powerful as contemporary exchanges.[2]

According to this the self's dialogues with God would turn out to be completely describable as the soul's interior dialogue with its memory of the interior dialogues of the ancient Hebrews as recorded in scripture, which dialogues of the ancient Hebrews were ultimately pinned to or got their content from events around the time of the Exodus which the acumen of the religious mind of Israel selected as revelatory. If this is the true description of our religious situation then prayer to be logical would turn out to be merely the person's meditation upon the idea of God constructed from the previous meditations of others upon certain humanly selected past events.

---

[1] SDH. p. 66cd. The quotation marks are Niebuhr's.
[2] SDH. p. 33bc.

It must not be thought that orthodox Christianity ignores the help given to us in our prayer life by dialogues with the past, either in the form of Scripture or of the continuing witness of the Church. What orthodox Christianity would claim about the prayer life is that, when the devout Christian is trying to know and obey God in daily life with the help of Scripture, the Holy Spirit himself aids directly within our lives by a selective illumination of Scripture and other sources of religious insight, and by strengthening us and giving us a selective illumination of our lives. This involves a real breaking of the creation barrier even though the divine work is usually carried out so slowly and quietly that most Christians most of the time cannot identify it at particular moments but only in its cumulative effect.

That Niebuhr does not really admit Deity's actual traffic with devout seekers is shown in remarks he makes about modern Judaism. "In the case of the Jewish nation," he says, "the power of common memories of a dim historic past is strong enough to preserve the cohesion of the nation although it lacked until recently a physical and geographic basis for its life."[1] Later he recurs to the same theme and says that the Jewish community of the Covenant has been maintained by "prophetic interpretations of the Covenant," "memories of critical historic events," "liturgical observances," and "the *Torah*."[2] The lack of mention of God's loving care and personal assistance is conspicuous. Niebuhr does not mean by this omission to suggest that Judaism has a lower status than Christianity in God's favor, for Niebuhr disapproves of Christian missionary activity among the Jews.[3]

The difficulty in writing about Niebuhr's theory of revelation is that he is a deeply religious man, to whom Biblical

---

[1] SDH. p. 40c.
[2] SDH. p. 87c-e.
[3] PSA. p. 108bc.

religion has been precious from his youth. In his personal life it simply seems that God must be personal and righteous.[1] So there are many times when in his description of personal religious experience he talks *as if* God's personality and righteousness were somehow part of the general revelation experienced direct in the human consciousness.

He says that "prophetism acknowledged . . . the personal encounter between God and man."[2] The word "encounter" is in itself in our use a word of very limited activity. It is only a word that brings the situation *up to the point for action.* Take for example this statement: "Returning home unexpectedly late at night, and switching on the light, he encountered a burglar in the act of stealing the teaspoons." No more of that incident is going to be told you. You are to be left for ever in the dark as to what the active interpersonal relationship between the burglar and the householder will be. The word "encounter" takes you up exactly to the threshold of that interpersonal relationship, *and not a step further.*[3] So too, when Niebuhr speaks of the "personal encounter between God and man" he is not in those words describing action relative to the other on the part of either. The only reason the reader *thinks* that Niebuhr is describing an active interpersonal relationship between God and man is because the reader brings to his reading his preconceived ideas of what happens after God and a man have encountered each other.

Another example of Niebuhr's seeming claim that specific knowledge about God's righteousness is directly transmitted to men through immediate communion with God is a statement he makes when he is describing historical theology. In this description he refers to "the mystery of the God whom the individual encountered in the final reaches of his self-

---

[1] This is the impression that one receives from his writings. I do not know Professor Niebuhr personally.

[2] SDH. p. 96b.

[3] Where "encounter" means "fight" other descriptive words are needed, as: one nation encountered another *in battle.*

awareness, where he met God as the 'other' who judged and forgave him."[1] It must be held in mind, however, that here Niebuhr is referring to what the Church as a historic fact has believed, without raising the question of whether this belief is as a matter of fact accurate. This is rather typical of Niebuhr. In the course of his writings he will occasionally digress at length upon what the Early Church believed or upon what Reformation Protestantism believed. Because this is sympathetically done it gives the impression of being all of a piece with the rest of his writing and creates an impression of more Orthodoxy than he actually subscribes to.

However, when he is speaking in his own person of what he believes to be true he goes so far as to say that "a religion of revelation is grounded in the faith that God speaks to man from beyond the highest pinnacle of the human spirit; and that this voice of God will discover man's highest not only to be short of the highest but involved in the dishonesty of claiming that it is the highest."[2] (Does this mean anything more than saying that man, when he seriously looks at his situation, realizes that he is not the whole show? "Higher" by itself is not an ethical word. It is spacial. If Niebuhr really means that a man hears the voice of God telling him that dishonesty is morally wrong, one wishes Niebuhr would state the idea clearly without using ambiguous expressions.) Niebuhr says that "An . . . important characteristic of the experience of God is the sense of being seen, commanded, judged and known from beyond ourselves."[3] But *what* is one commanded to do? *How* is one judged? Little help is derived from Niebuhr's explanation that "The soul which reaches the outermost rims of its own consciousness, must also come in contact with God, for He impinges upon that consciousness."[4] The word "impinge"

---

[1] SDH. p. 96a. Quotation marks Niebuhr's.
[2] (1)HN. p. 203b.
[3] (1)HN. p. 128b.
[4] (1)HN. p. 127ef.

implies a mechanical striking. It is not a word of spiritual communication or interpersonal communion. We are brought a little closer to the heart of the matter by the claim that "In personal life the moral experience consists of the sense of moral obligation as being laid upon man not by himself, nor yet by his society but by God."[1]

> The general revelation of personal human experience, the sense of being confronted with a 'wholly other' at the edge of human consciousness, contains three elements, two of which are not too sharply defined, while the third is not defined at all. The first is the sense of reverence for a majesty and of dependence upon an ultimate source of being. The second is the sense of moral obligation laid upon one from beyond oneself and of moral unworthiness before a judge. The third, most problematic of the elements in religious experience, is the longing for forgiveness. All three of these elements become more sharply defined as they gain the support of other forms of revelation.[2]

It is the second of these three elements that is strategically important for our discussion. If Niebuhr took this statement at face value and really geared his whole thought to the belief that God in general revelation reveals himself directly to our consciences as morally demanding and as judge, then he would be admitting activity across the creation barrier on the part of God in general revelation. For general revelation would then have an ideational content of a sort to have a specifically directing effect upon a man's life. Hence Niebuhr would be admitting miracle, which is the watershed between Orthodoxy and Liberalism.

But what Niebuhr has admitted with the right hand of religious fervor he immediately takes away with the left hand of intellectual skepticism because he insists that this "universal human experience, the sense of being commanded,

---

[1] (1) HN. p. 137a.
[2] (1) HN. p. 131d-f.

placed under obligation and judged" is "conscience,"[1] and is only *"interpreted* as a relation between God and man in which it is God who makes demands and judgments upon man."[2] For "without the principle of interpretation furnished by . . . 'special revelation,' " . . . i.e, "specific historical events (which) become special revelations of the character of God and of His purposes," . . . "the general experience or the general revelation involved in conscience becomes falsified, because it is explained merely as man facing the court of social approval or disapproval or as facing his own 'best self.' "[3] . . . "The God whom we meet as 'The Other' at the final limit of our own consciousness, is not fully known to us except as specific revelations of His character [i.e., specific historical events] augment this general experience of being confronted from beyond ourselves."[4] This is an all out attempt to give the impression of actual traffic between the supernatural Deity and ourselves without really admitting it to be a fact. Niebuhr never really deviates from the position that "a general revelation can only point to the reality of God but not to His particular attributes."[5]

---

[1] (1) HN. pp. 128f, 129ab.

[2] (1) HN. p. 129b. Italics mine. And note that Niebuhr here as elsewhere refers to "man" as an abstract generalization, not to "a man" who is a specific and a concrete individual. This is part of Niebuhr's whole general inability to describe God as an uncreated spiritual being coming into an interpersonal relationship with a man who is a created spiritual being.

[3] (1) HN. p. 130ef.

[4] (1) HN. p. 130de.

[5] BT. p. 15de.

CHAPTER VI

GOD'S LACK OF ASSISTANCE TO MEN:
JESUS AND THE HOLY SPIRIT

FOR NIEBUHR CHRIST is the revelation *par excellence,* the point at which man fully sees the basic character of God.[1] The Old Testament had said that God is a God of justice and mercy, and had stressed justice primarily. It had always found difficulty in showing how God's mercy relates to his justice.[2] The crucifixion of Christ, and Niebuhr stresses nothing but the crucifixion and barely mentions in passing the ministry of the human Jesus, shows the centrality of God's love and relates it to his justice and wrath.[3] This makes Christ the final revelation, for he is the complete solution of the centuries old problem of the prophets.[4] The Law had furthermore shown itself inadequate to deal with the recalcitrance of the human heart, which in its subtleties can still make itself the center of interests and ambitions and can even make use of law to that end.[5] Christ makes clear that God "has resources of love and redemption transcending His judgments"[6] which can "triumph over the recalcitrance of human sin."[7] In this sense also he is the final revelation.[8]

---

[1] FH. p. 33fg; FH. p. 27de.
[2] (1) HN. p. 132bc.
[3] (1) HN. pp. 142e, 143ab.
[4] (1) HN. p. 132bc; (2) HD. p. 55def.
[5] FH. p. 194bc; (1) HN. p. 147ab.
[6] (1) HN. p. 143cd.
[7] FH. p. 169f.
[8] (1) HN. p. 142c.

We saw in the previous chapter that for Niebuhr there are two kinds of revelation, general and particular. The general one is the diffused sense that man has that beyond the outermost reach of his own being there is a Divine Being. This general feeling has content read into it as man sees certain particular events in history as revelatory of the character of God. The content of revelation is wholly defined by the particular revelations, that is by certain specific events in history which the prophetic mind selects and judges to be revelatory of God's character.[1] These revelatory events are entirely enmeshed in the cause and effect sequences of the natural order. Revelation for Niebuhr never involves a breaking of the creation barrier.[2] The closest Niebuhr comes to it is in his theory of general revelation in which the human soul, in the outermost reaches of its being, is aware that there is a God beyond itself. However, the divine here referred to is described as completely static.[3] It or He never does anything to a man. The action, if any, is all on the man's part. And as the God of general revelation is described as known as an overtone to all human experience man is not described as knowing the God of general revelation by doing certain things or seeking him in a particular way or as *feeling Him* in particular events.

It should be noted that a God who made himself *felt* in particular events and not in others would be a God who broke the creation barrier with a revelation that had intellectual content. When children play hide and seek a great deal of information can be given the seeker by simply telling him whether he is "hot" or "cold." In fact, much of the education of young children is carried on by the simple formula, "Mamma says No," which prunes the infant's exuberant random activity into a socially artistic growth. But general revelation for Niebuhr contains no specific visitations of

---

[1] FH. p. 141cd; FH. p. 144ab.
[2] CRPP. p. 198bc; FH. p. 142cd.
[3] (1) HN. p. 142ef.

the Divine. He has a completely non-miraculous theory of revelation.

In understanding Niebuhr's theory of Christ, the great revelation, the key lies entirely in what has been said of Niebuhr's theory of Old Testament revelation. He conforms to it his whole position on the relation of Jesus to God, the nature of the Atonement, the question of the Resurrection of Jesus, and the nature of the salvation attained for man.

The implicit presupposition upon which Niebuhr's thought is actually moving at this point is not stressed. But he really is proceeding upon the implicit assumption that the stream cannot rise higher than its source.[1] "Therefore the highest human excellencies are clues to the character of God."[2] He has believed that God is righteous and that "the highest justice of God is the holiness of His love."[3] From this he concludes that, since Jesus at his crucifixion is the highest and most perfect example of love that we know, the crucifixion must reveal to us more perfectly than anything else the nature of God.[4] This is a line of reasoning which, if pushed to its logical conclusion, involves the belief in the Resurrection, in life after death, and in the assistance of the Holy Spirit in human life. But Niebuhr refuses to push the logic of this belief the whole way and hold its corollaries on faith, trusting that in the future a better working harmony of these ideas with science will be found than has hitherto been the case. Instead, as soon as his belief in God's goodness reaches a point at which its practical implications seem to run counter to the current philosophy of science, he retreats from the idea of goodness as the guiding thread of his theological reasoning in order to present a view more easily harmonized with current science-conditioned philosophy.

---

[1] DCNR. p. 237a.
[2] CPP. p. 197bcd.
[3] (2) HD. p. 56e; REE. p. 285b.
[4] (1) HN. pp. 143ef, 144a; DCNR. p. 237a-c.

Thus, true to his basic belief that the creation barrier is never broken, Niebuhr does not believe that Jesus Christ is the literal Incarnation of Deity. He considers the doctrine of the two natures of Christ religiously helpful but verging on logical nonsense.[1] He thinks the teaching about the virgin birth was an afterthought in early Christianity that indicated a weakening of the faith.[2] For Niebuhr Jesus was "a Jewish teacher, rabbi, and prophet who made messianic claims for himself."[3] He was fully and exclusively human and since he was tempted in the wilderness and later,[4] and since to be tempted means in some sense to have sinned (according to Niebuhr), complete sinlessness cannot be predicated of him.[5] All that can be said of him is that there was in Jesus "a remarkable coincidence and consistency of doctrine, of purpose and of act."[6]

Unlike other men, who, even the best of them, have two foci of interest that guide their action, the love of God and the love of themselves, Jesus has "an uncompromising insistence upon conformity to God's will."[7] Actually Niebuhr does not make much of the warmth of Christ's human love. This is because the day by day details of his ministry and his human friendships are ignored. In reality it is those teachings and actions that make Jesus seem loving to us. The reason Christianity through the centuries has seen the crucifixion as the supreme example of his love is that the crucifixion eternally authenticates and transfigures the love we see in his actions and teaching. In other words if we knew nothing of the ministry of Jesus and so could not bring to the crucifixion a portrait of his character and personality, the crucifixion would not reveal his love for us as

---

[1] (2)HD. pp. 60e-61b; (2)HD. pp. 70cd, 71ab; (1)HN. p. 145cd; FH. pp. 33fg, 34a; DCNR. p. 236bc; DCNR. p. 80a-c; SDH. p. 96d.
[2] FH. p. 148a; CRPP. p. 198bc.
[3] FH. p. 142cd; BT. p. 177ef; (2)HD. p. 45ab.
[4] Matthew 4:1-11; Luke 22:28.
[5] (1)HN. p. 251a; (2)HD. p. 73e; DST. p. 166.
[6] (2)HD. p. 73f.
[7] (2)HD. p. 73f.

it now does. Thousands of men were crucified in the Roman world who were not revelations of God.

According to Niebuhr, Jesus followed God's love exactly and so refused to protect himself by using the sinful exertion of power in his own behalf, which would have given him worldly safety at the price of increasing the pressure of exploitation upon the weak.[1] When he refused to play the game according to the world's standards it was inevitable that the selfish pressures of the world would crucify him.[2] But his crucifixion became our highest revelation of the love of God.[3] In the Cross God himself is seen to suffer in love because of and on behalf of man's sin.[4] Since Niebuhr denies the Incarnation with its claim that Christ Jesus is literally the God-man,[5] the only way it is possible to get from the death of a human being on Golgotha to the idea of God's suffering love is by arguing that, since the stream cannot rise higher than its source, the highest human expression of love that we know must be a revelation of the character of God.[6]

To stop at this point, however, is to make Jesus of Nazareth merely the supreme example of the Suffering Servant. Niebuhr, in line with Orthodoxy, does make much of Jesus as the supreme example of the Suffering Servant.[7] But for Orthodoxy Jesus is more than the Suffering Servant. Niebuhr also would like to think of Jesus as more, but his theory of revelation and his lack of belief in a genuine Incarnation do not give him logical grounds for ascribing a larger role to Jesus in the crucifixion. So at this point, wanting spiritually to say more than he logically can say, Niebuhr's writing becomes blurred, implying more than he really subscribes to. For unless one is reading carefully one may be unaware

---

1 (2)HD. p. 72ab; BT. p. 177ef.
2 ICE. p. 54abc; BT. p. 177ef.
3 FH. p. 144ab; DCNR. p. 237; REE. p. 287cd.
4 (2)HD. p. 46ab; (2)HD. p. 56a; DST. p. 177a-c.
5 FH. pp. 33fg, 34a; REE. p. 279bc.
6 FH. p. 169f. But the Cross here is only "the symbolic point."
7 BT. pp. 192d-f, 193ab; DST. pp. 3ef, 4a; (1)HN. pp. 143f, 144a; (2) HD. p. 46a.

that Niebuhr is not talking about the incarnate Second Person of the Godhead. "The perfection of Christ" is "the transcendent *agape* symbolized in the Cross."[1] "The Jesus of history," he says elsewhere in more obvious language, "actually created the Christ of faith in the life of the early Church."[2]

The benefits that the crucifixion makes possible for man can be entirely summed up under the heading of revelation and the consequences in human life as man reacts to the revelation. God's love for man Niebuhr thinks of as intuitively deducible from the crucifixion. The death of Jesus is the perfect "symbol" of the divine love.[3] (It is not the loving God in action, for that of course would involve a breaking of the creation barrier.) It is a symbol also of the Divine will.[4] Man, when he is confronted by the crucifixion, is made aware of the heinousness of his own sin.[5] This awareness initiates repentance.[6] The state of repentance is synonymous with redemption.[7] Thus what twentieth century men *do* when they meditate upon what a *first century man endured* brings about the state of salvation. Only human action is involved.[8] There is no claim that when men repent the supernatural God does something to them personally which brings about the state of salvation, for that would involve a breaking of the creation barrier.

In Niebuhr's thought we see in Jesus the Divine love that can only enter history to suffer defeat.[9] God has power and love, but since power in the earthly scene always is involved in moral corruption, the Divine love, when it enters

---

[1] (2) HD. p. 81f.
[2] ICE. p. 120d; FH. pp. 33fg, 34a.
[3] REE. p. 287b-d; FH. pp. 143f, 144a; DST. p. 144ab.
[4] FH. p. 238a; DST. p. 140b-f.
[5] (1) HN. p. 148a; FH. p. 144b; (2) HD. p. 46c; (2) HD. p. 56f.
[6] ICE. pp. 120f, 121a; FH. pp. 142fg, 143a; FH. p. 149bc; (2) HD. pp. 56ef, 57a; DST. p. 147a-d.
[7] REE. pp. 294f, 295abef; REE. p. 285cd; CRPP. p. 111bc.
[8] (2) HD. pp. 56f, 57ab.
[9] BT. pp. 177ef, 178a; DST. p. 144b.

history must show itself as goodness without power.[1] We must be careful not to read more into this statement than Niebuhr allows. *The Divine entering history* sounds superficially as if it means God breaking the creation barrier to become truly incarnate. Niebuhr seems to wish to convey an aura of this Orthodox meaning to himself as well as to the reader, but what he means by *the Divine entering history* is only *the emergence from private life into public ministry of a man whose love fully symbolizes the Divine love.*[2] When this suffering love of God is fully symbolized on earth we have the "Christ event."[3] The crucifixion of Jesus is therefore the "Christ event."[4] All outstanding human instances of sacrificial love symbolize God's love to some extent.[5] The crucifixion of Jesus symbolizes it most perfectly.[6] Professor Carnell remarks in commenting on Niebuhr that:

> The Jesus of history appears merely to be a convenient locus to pin the Christ symbol to, for He was simply more consistent in his *agape* living than others. But one must note that if Socrates had been more consistent in his life and a little more successful in his oracular contacts with eternity, he could just as well serve as the symbol of our faith. Our faith would then be the 'Socratic faith,' and our hope, not the cross, but 'the flask of hemlock.' Jesus was just more consistent in his conformity to the will of God than was either Socrates or Gandhi; but He, not less than they, was a sinner.[7]

---

[1] (2)HD. p. 72ab; BT. p. 155c; BT. pp. 167ef, 168a; BT. p. 185cd.

[2] FH. pp. 33fg, 34a; REE. p. 287cdf; DST. p. 144ab; FH. pp. 143fg, 144a; (2)HD. p. 72a.

[3] SDH. p. 91de.

[4] LNTC. p. 102a-d; SDH. p. 91def.

[5] LNTC. p. 102a-d; CPP. p. 37de.

[6] DCNR. p. 237a-c.

[7] Edward J. Carnell, *The Theology of Reinhold Niebuhr* (Grand Rapids: Wm. B. Eerdmans Publishing Company, 1951), p. 155. And see (2)HD. p. 73def.

When we ask what is the sequel to the crucifixion in the personal career of Jesus of Nazareth Niebuhr's answer is that there is no sequel. "Jesus is, superficially considered, a tragic figure."[1] "The perfect love of the life of Christ ends on the Cross."[2] Niebuhr follows the Hebrew conception of man as a soul-body organism, so the idea of a spiritual soul escaping at death from a physical body has to be foreign to his belief.[3] And as he rejects miracles as contrary to the teaching of science he admits that he has difficulty with the physical resurrection of Jesus.[4] This leaves him only two alternatives. Either he has to believe that our memories of Jesus are the only life Jesus now has, or else he has to believe that the resurrection of Jesus of Nazareth from the dead has not yet taken place but will occur at some time in the future.[5] Since Niebuhr speaks of all people as "perishing" at death, the latter alternative seems to be ruled out.[6] He certainly believes that Jesus to date has not risen as an individual,[7] and there is certainly no statement in his writings claiming that either Jesus of Nazareth or other individuals will have a postponed resurrection some time in the future. That is, Niebuhr's thought does not revert to the pre-Christian Jewish conception of resurrection as something that will take place at some future date when "many of those who sleep in the dust of the earth shall awake, some to everlasting life, and some to shame and everlasting contempt."[8]

---

[1] BT. p. 155d; ICE. pp. 120f, 121a; BT. p. 192de; (2) HD. p. 81cd.

[2] (1) HN. p. 164b.

[3] SDH. pp. 237f-238a; BT. p. 188def; CRPP. p. 198bc.

[4] CRPP. p. 198bcef; SDH. p. 91de; SDH. p. 237a. And see ICE. p. 216ab. This rejects "St. Paul's Christ-mysticism" and reduces "the living Christ" to "a dimension of life." FH. p. 147bc. This indicates that the resurrection story was originally concocted by the disciples as a symbol of their faith. FH. pp. 147de, 148abc. It is the "revelatory depth" of the resurrection rather than the resurrection itself which is important.

[5] BT. p. 188def; SDH. p. 237cde.

[6] (2) HD. p. 308c.

[7] FH. p. 176bc. Christ's triumph over death is merely "emancipation from anxiety about death."

[8] Daniel 12:2.

This original Jewish doctrine of the resurrection would as inescapably involve a breaking of the creation barrier as do the Orthodox Christian doctrines of the Incarnation and the Resurrection of Christ. Niebuhr only describes Christ's Resurrection as the influence upon his followers of their memory of the historical Jesus.[1]

It is odd that Niebuhr should seem so unconcerned about the personal fate of Jesus. *Any* demand that there *ought* to be a life after death Niebuhr tends to shrug off impatiently as "a transcendental version of the old sin of trying too desperately to live."[2] The retort to this always is that the demand that *we* have a *right* to live happily after this life may be sinful self assertion, but for us to demand that Jesus of Nazareth had a *right* to live happily after death is not sinful self assertion, it is only demanding mere elementary justice from God.

We have pointed out earlier that one of the remarkable things about Jewish religion was the ability of the great leaders to have such confidence in the righteousness of God that they were unafraid to question him when his ways seemed unrighteous. The two most famous instances of this are Jeremiah and Job. Jeremiah asked God why the way of the wicked prospers, and received an answer that underneath its figurative language merely implied that the prophet had better "buck up" because he had greater difficulties ahead of him.[3] Job's question is the reverse side of Jeremiah's. Job asks God why he suffers, being good, and in the end God, while not contradicting Job's claim to righteousness, silences him by simply overwhelming him with the unsearchable divine greatness, so that he is willing and able to take his mind off of himself and adore God. The writer of the book of Job is not altogether satisfied with God's answer and adds as a kind of crude footnote to the story the statement that after Job's trials he had a great deal of

---

[1] MMIS. p. 263de.
[2] FH. p. 176c; FH. p. 63d.
[3] Jeremiah 12:1,5.

worldly and family prosperity. There is no attempt at elevated thought or poetic language in this concluding note. It is as if the writer were saying, "I am no more satisfied with this postscript as an answer to Job's problem than you are, earnest reader. I just want to go on record as saying that I am not altogether satisfied with the rather cavalier answer the Almighty gave Job."

We cannot think from the Gospel record that Jesus was ever troubled by doubts about the heavenly Father's love and righteousness, although at the end of the crucifixion he felt estranged from that love. Neither did he ever think of himself as championing his people against God as Moses did in the incident of the golden calf.[1] Jesus constantly thought of himself as working for and with God on behalf of men. And yet, while Jesus did not himself put to God the question of Jeremiah and Job, nevertheless in the eyes of his followers his death does put the old question and this time puts it not in the form of a question but in the form of a demand bid, a challenge that even Almighty God dare not ignore if he expects men to believe that he is righteous. The reputation of Almighty God is at stake in the Resurrection.

Jesus before his crucifixion spoke of his death as a giving of "his life as a ransom for many,"[2] as if he believed that the death itself would have a kind of potency. The old view of human sacrifice was that in an emergency it was a desperate measure that was extremely potent in securing divine aid. Hence Jephthah's vow,[3] and the great wrath that came upon Israel and forced their army to withdraw when the king of Moab offered his eldest son as a burnt offering upon the wall.[4] The prophets did well in opposing human sacrifice but it continued to be practised among the Hebrew people as late as the time of Jeremiah.

---

[1] Exodus 32:11-14.
[2] Mark 10:45.
[3] Judges 10:9; 11:30,31.
[4] II Kings 3:26,27.

Jesus expected that in his crucifixion his adversaries would inadvertently make him the supreme sacrifice to further the welfare of God's kingdom.

Judaism had claimed that God is both powerful and righteous, and we have seen that the height of righteousness involves active outgoing love for others.[1] It was an idea that first came into full focus in prophetic thought with Hosea. When Jesus' followers look at him they look at a life so perfect in its devotion to God that if God let it be snuffed out at death one could deny that God felt any respect for human personality or was characterized by practical outgoing love toward Jesus, and if he would not show love toward Jesus, the chances are entirely against his showing love toward anybody. It must be remembered that love and respect for personality are relations between *individuals*. One cannot have the characteristic of either love or respect for personality without practising love and respect for personality toward individuals. A God who would leave Jesus in the lurch at Calvary would not be a God of love. Furthermore, God would not even be just in the simpler legalistic sense of the term.

The question of whether God would have had power to help Jesus does not arise. For the word God means by definition the Omnipotent Power. There is power in the universe so somewhere there must be the greatest power. One can question whether the greatest power is righteous, conscious, or purposive, but not that the greatest power exists. If therefore God is thought of as righteous and loving and as respecting human personality, those concepts are something added to the concept of power, even though it is believed that God's power is invariably under the direction of his loving-righteous purpose. The idea of Ultimate Power is inherent in the concept of God. One can of course define the Ultimate Power—in view of science—as something that necessarily runs on undeviating schedule and so cannot make

---

[1] (2) HD. p. 56de.

special arrangement for any individual. But love does make special arrangements for individuals. A business magnate whose life ran on such undeviating schedule that he could not take time out to be interested when his small son made the third grade baseball team or could not take time out to send his wife flowers on their wedding anniversary would be thought deficient in love. Righteous love by definition makes personal arrangements for individuals. One has a right to say that in view of the discoveries of science one has been forced to accept as one's God a Power that is other than the Jewish-Christian conception of God-as-guiding-his-Omnipotent-Power-by-his-Righteous-Loving-Purpose; but one has no right to worship the Ideal-of-Righteous-Loving-Purpose and claim that he is worshipping a God when in reality he is adoring an abstraction. Neither has a person a right to worship Power shorn of the attributes of righteous-loving-purpose and claim that he is worshipping the Jewish-Christian God. Neither has one a right to claim that either brute matter, or in more modern parlance the interlocking ongoing event, is other than God as part of the original *given,* and then give this as an excuse for God's inability to fully cope with matter, or the interlocking ongoing event, to bring it fully into line with his righteous-loving purpose. For this theory takes much of the ultimate power away from the Divine Spirit to place it in matter or the interlocking ongoing event. This makes the Divine Spirit not God but a Demiurge, and so is contrary to the Jewish-Christian religion. One can honestly be merely a Platonist. One cannot honestly be merely a Platonist and claim to be a Christian. One can honestly give up Christianity. One cannot honestly pretend to keep Christianity and give up the description of God as Omnipotent-Power-directed-by-Righteous-Loving-Purpose.

Jesus had kept the law and in addition had poured out his life in lavish devotion to God. As Jesus' parables take for granted, human masters of not spectacular virtue are accustomed to reward faithful service.[1] If God could not even live up to a decent human standard in this regard in his relation to Jesus he would not be righteous. He would not deserve man's service. For man ought to serve only the good.

"The essential principle of spiritual authority is the evocation by Good of appreciation of itself; for only when this occurs is authority exercised over the spirit."[2] Using scientific jargon at this point, the ministry plus the death of Jesus constitute man's "controlled experiment" as to the character of God. For friendship is an interpersonal relationship and here all the requisite human advances and adjustments to such a relationship had been perfectly made. Friends do not needlessly leave their friends badly in the lurch. The ancient Hebrews had always vindicated the character of the Almighty at the expense of cheerfully shouldering the heavy burden of human guilt as an explanation of why an all powerful righteous God should allow his chosen nation to undergo so much suffering. It was not, they said, because of any lack of desire to be friends with them and cherish them and respect them on the part of Omnipotence, but simply because as utterly pure he could not tie himself in with their moral evil in bonds of friendship. But Jesus had fulfilled the law. His was a life with which the Eternal Holy One could enter into a relation of supporting comradeship with no derogation to his moral perfection. Hence if, at Calvary and after, the Creator turned down the opportunity to use his powerfully assisting friendship to make the man Jesus triumph joyously, and if the Creator callously neglected to say an adequate "thank you" to the human Jesus for his life and death of undeviating loyal service, then we know that God is not righteous and that He does not love men or value their costly devotion to him.

Jesus' whole ethic as we see it in his teaching is based

---

[1] Matthew 24:45-47; 25:14-23; Luke 12:35-44; 19:12-19.
[2] William Temple, *Nature, Man and God* (London: Macmillan, 1951), p. 345.

upon the belief that the all powerful heavenly Father is dependably righteous and loving. So there is a more intimate connection between the Resurrection and the ethics of Jesus than is usually realized. For if Jesus perished at Calvary the claim that he is a great moral teacher is false, because the basic presupposition of his ethic is shown to be untrue. If Buddha's insight into the nature of Ultimate Being and man's relation to It is the correct one, then Buddha is a greater ethical teacher than Jesus, because Buddha gave wise counsels as to human interpersonal relationships in view of the actual nature of Ultimate Reality, while all Jesus' suggestions about human interpersonal relationships stem from a basic illusion about the nature of Ultimate Reality.

In this discussion the word "Resurrection" is used as meaning at least that the Divine-Human Jesus continues to exist after Easter as a living individual with enormously heightened power and with complete continuity of personal memory that includes both his earthly life and his after-Easter heavenly existence, and that since this risen Christ is fully human as well as Divine, human beings since Easter have had available through him a more adequate permanent contact with God than was previously generally available. To use the word "Resurrection" in relation to Jesus with any lessened implication is an illegitimate juggling of terms. Jesus' Resurrection may very possibly involve a great deal more than this. It cannot involve less without nullifying the entire "good news" of the "gospel."

Many people who have felt unable to believe in this kind of a Resurrection, which is admittedly miraculous, have tried to retreat to an acceptance of Jesus as the world's greatest ethical teacher, and to a definition of his immortality as merely the perpetuation of his influence due to the Church's historical memory of his ministry and death. But without his Resurrection as a living individual human person he is shown not to be the world's greatest ethical teacher, because his ethic is undercut when God is seen not to show active supporting love to cherish the existence of a human individual who has perfectly served him. For Jesus' whole ethic rests upon the assumption that God is a loving Father. And no omnipotent loving Father would abandon such a son as Jesus.[1]

In trying to analyse the thought and mind of Jesus it cannot be too often said that his method of teaching was that of a religious popularizer and that the way his mind worked was different from that of the typical graduate school student or professor of the twentieth century. What we have in the synoptic gospels is a collection of significant incidents from the life of Jesus, plus the collection of short sayings that were the distillation of his thought, plus the parables which were the distilled repertoire of his illustrative material. As a veteran teacher of teen-age students I know from experience that in popularizing difficult material for inexperienced minds one acquires both a repertoire of statements that are a neat packaging of important ideas, and a repertoire of anecdotal illustrative material.[2]

What the person who has not been engaged in popularization does not realize is that the items in these distillations represent not so much particular ideas in the teacher's thought as they do the active intersection of many ideas, the creative crossroads to which many lines of thought converge and from which many lines of thought lead out. Thus in Jesus' teaching the use of the parable of the Lost Sheep to illustrate in Luke[3] that there is joy in heaven over one sinner who repents, and in Matthew[4] that it is not the will of God that one of these little children should perish probably reflects Jesus' own double use of the anecdote. The parables are neither hard and fast allegories that can be crystallized into doctrinal statements, nor are they each a

---

[1] Matthew 7:11.

[2] In my own case my book *Theology You Can Understand* (New York: Morehouse-Gorham Co., 1956), is the systematizing of these statements and anecdotes.

[3] Luke 15:3-7.

[4] Matthew 18:10-14.

story making merely a single point. The ease with which they lend themselves to various homiletic uses is an indication that in their original use by Jesus they were emergences from his total perception of God's relationship to men.

As Jesus' mind played with certain great themes there arose certain pictures that reappear in various forms in many of his teachings. One of these is the scene of the return or homecoming.[1]

The most outstanding example of this is Jesus' greatest parable, the story of the Prodigal Son.[2] The figure of the father in this story has generally been considered Jesus' greatest thumbnail sketch of the character of God. The miserable prodigal left the security and love of his father's house and wandered into a far country where to all Jewish hearers it was obvious that true holiness was not appreciated: men kept pigs! At last battered and spent he returned home from that country. His father was watching for his return and gave him a royal welcome: the kiss, the ring, the shoes, the best robe, and the feast with the fatted calf, music, and dancing. This was because his son "was dead, and is alive again." One suspects that deep in Jesus' consciousness there was a connection between this fictitious homecoming and the homecoming to the Heavenly Father that he must have expected for himself, in view of the fact that he believed he would eventually sit at the right hand of Power, and come with the clouds of heaven.[3]

If Jesus was correct in his belief that the love of God is so great that he gives to returning sinners the royal welcome implied in the Prodigal Son parable, what kind of a welcome could God have been expected to give Jesus when he returned to the Father on Good Friday, more footsore

---

[1] Matthew 25:1-30; Mark 12:1-11; 13:34-37; Luke 11:5-13; 12:41-48; 15:3-6; 15:11-32; 19:11-27.

[2] Luke 15:11-32.

[3] Mark 14:61,62. We know that at least some other of his parables contain in their undercurrent an association with thoughts of his personal career. Mark 11:30-12:12 and Luke 16:19-31 especially vv. 27-31.

and broken by his journey into the far country of sinful men than the selfish spendthrift had ever been by his life among the pigs? If God did not raise Jesus from the dead to everlasting joyous companionship with himself, then Jesus was simply mistaken in his understanding of the character of God. And so the ethic that he preached is foundationless, for the type of life he counsels men to live is advised on the presupposition that it is permanently supported by the all powerful Heavenly Father.

And this undermines also Niebuhr's claim for a valid place for Christianity in twentieth century life, for Niebuhr follows the logic of ethics as having priority over the logic of metaphysics in his thought. He has claimed to return to Biblical religion. He urges men to give their lives in selfless devotion to others in fulfillment of the command to love thy neighbor as thyself. He thinks that although the good man perishes himself in so doing he has the satisfaction of knowing that the personality of others is conserved by his suffering loyalty unto death to ethical values. But if the universe does not conserve *his* personality, neither will it conserve the personalities of those he has sacrificed himself to assist. Niebuhr says:

> Religion in its purest form does not guarantee man an immediate reward for every ethical achievement; indeed it may offer him no reward at all except the reward which inheres in the act itself. But it does give him the final satisfaction of guaranteeing the reality of a universe which is not blind to the values for which he must pay such a high price, and which is not indifferent or hostile to his struggle. It asks him to respect human personality because the universe itself, in spite of some obvious evidence to the contrary, knows how to conserve personality.[1]

But human beings are able to enhance other human personalities only to a slight extent and certainly completely

---

[1] DCNR. pp. 49f-50c.

lack the power to conserve other human personalities permanently. For personality can only be conserved by conserving the person. Otherwise what you would have would only be the temporary conservation of the memory of personalities in lives that succeed them. And that memory is shorter than we like to admit. Do you know even the maiden names of your four great-grandmothers? If personality is to be conserved ultimately, it must be conserved by Ultimate Reality's conservation of the personality bearing person. And if Jesus was not raised from the dead then the religious evidence is that Ultimate Reality is uninterested in the conservation of personality, and so the whole case for Christianity is destroyed, and with it the foundation upon which Niebuhr builds his theology and ethics. For he claims theologically that the Christ event of Calvary reveals suffering love in the heart of God, which it does not do if God is completely callous to the suffering of Jesus. And it undercuts his ethics which demands as the fulfillment of our obedience to the will of God, the all out self-forgetful attempt to conserve the personality of other people.

Of course the Church was founded on the belief that the Resurrection followed the crucifixion. So supreme joy followed for Jesus the pain of Good Friday. St. Paul is right in claiming that if the Resurrection did not take place the Christian hope is in vain.[1] Coming to the same conclusion from a different angle William Temple says:

> That historical life [of Christ] is so intimately one with the eternal which it makes manifest, that if it could be annihilated, the eternal would be different in quality. . . . As in order of historical development, so also in order of spiritual value, the hope of immortality is strictly dependent on and subordinate to faith in God. If God is righteous,—still more, if God is Love —immortality follows as a consequence. He made me;

---

[1] I Corinthians 15.

He loves me; He will not let me perish, so long as there is in me anything that he can love.[1]

The moral character of the Christian God is at stake in the resurrection of Jesus.

It is instructive to note the extensive use Reinhold Niebuhr makes of the parable of the Prodigal Son in his essay, "The Christian Church in a Secular Age":[2]

> The whole story of modern culture [says Niebuhr] might be truly chronicled in terms of the Parable of the Prodigal Son. The more rationalistic humanism is the son in the first stages of his emancipation from his father. . . . The more romantic type of modern humanism, as revealed in the religio-political movements of the Continent, represent[s] a more advanced state of disintegration. Here the son is 'wasting his substance in riotous living.' . . . The 'mighty famine' when the son begins to be in want is still in the future,[3] but our civilization is destined for such a catastrophe. . . . The real difficulty of preaching the gospel of God's mercy to the prodigal son, our modern culture, lies in the temptation to play the part of the elder brother in the Lord's Parable. . . . A profane Christianity, like the elder brother, ostensibly manifests its sense of dependence upon the Father, but it uses this relationship to satisfy a sinful egotism. . . . Since the historic Church is always touched with human finiteness . . . any tendency to obscure or deny this fact becomes the final and most terrible expression of human sinfulness. Of that sin no Church has been free.[4]

Niebuhr's entire interest is centered upon the differing sins of the two sons. In the use he makes of the parable there

---

[1] William Temple, *Nature, Man and God* (London: Macmillan, 1951), pp. 448ab, 457e.
[2] In CPP.
[3] Written in 1937.
[4] CPP. pp. 208, 209, 217, 218.

is no description of the practical specific activity of the father's outgoing love. The father is not an active participant in the story. This in itself is only significant because it is typical of all of Niebuhr's writing. One looks in vain in his books for descriptions of specific actions on the part of God relative to the world and men. Niebuhr does say here, "The real difficulty in preaching the gospel of God's mercy to the prodigal son . . . ," thereby giving the impression that he does believe the father's part in the story and that it is something that he deals with at length elsewhere in his writings. But when one searches those writings to find specific instances of God's mercy one discovers that they turn out to be "processes of nature and history."[1]

For Niebuhr cannot describe God's outgoing love because the fellowship between the soul and God initiated by the divine *agape* Love is an interpersonal relationship which would have to involve God's breaking the creation barrier, inasmuch as man is part of the creation and God is not. This is an event which Niebuhr believes to be an impossibility. The *agape* love of the human Jesus he believes to be merely analogous to the Divine Love,[2] and the sight of Jesus' self sacrificing love fully reveals the seriousness of man's sin,[3] making man "aware of the character of his self-love and its incompatibility with the divine will."[4] "It is by that knowledge that man is brought to despair."[5] But since the death of Christ is also a symbol of the divine love "remorse" can "be transmuted into repentance."[6] "When the sinful self is broken . . . the real self is fulfilled from beyond itself,"[7] but not from beyond the creation according to the tenor of Niebuhr's teaching.

---

[1] See *ante,* pp. 75, 76.

[2] LNTC. p. 85e; REE. p. 287c; BT. p. 23ef; (2) HD. pp. 68c, 72cd. Jesus' love merely symbolizes the Divine Love because in Niebuhr's theology Jesus Christ is not literally the God-Man, supernatural Deity incarnate.

[3] (2) HD. p. 56f.

[4] (2) HD. p. 122a.

[5] (2) HD. p. 56f.

[6] (1) HN. p. 257d.

[7] (2) HD. p. 113d.

Under the heading *Grace as the Forgiveness of Our Sins*[1] Niebuhr points out that it is experience which validates man's experience in the confrontation of the Cross: "Repentance does initiate a new life."[2] But Niebuhr's language when analyzed shows God to be inactive in relation to men:[3] It is the man's *repentance* that initiates the new life, not *God* who initiates the new life when the man repents. Furthermore the "new life" that Niebuhr speaks of as being initiated is not the regenerated or reborn life of traditional Christian belief. For generation to take place in the merely worldly sense of the word something from beyond the mother must be added to her powers to produce the offspring. In the traditional Christian use of the words regeneration and rebirth the implication is that some power direct from Deity has been added to the ordinary human life to bring a new life into being. The words regeneration and rebirth when used in their traditional Christian sense involve God's breaking the creation barrier to modify the being of a particular human person. Instead of this, in Niebuhr's thought the "new life" is a "reconstruction of the self." To reconstruct is to reassemble old materials in a new fashion. But only the old materials are involved. Nothing new has been added. Niebuhr says, "The possibility of a reconstruction of the self is felt to be the consequence of 'power' and 'grace'[4] from beyond itself."[5] But even here he only seems to be expressing the traditional Christian belief. For he puts the words " 'power' " and " 'grace' " in quotation marks to show that he is not using the words in their traditional sense but only in his own redefined symbolic sense. In this merely symbolic sense they cannot of course effect a genuine causation. He does not

---

[1] (2) HD. p. 119c.
[2] (2) HD. p. 122a.
[3] For the sad carry-over of this into the wide cultural realm see SNE. pp. 135b-136a.
[4] In both cases the quotation marks are Niebuhr's.
[5] (2) HD. p. 110bc.

say they *cause* a reconstruction of the self. He only implies that the reconstruction of the self is a "consequence" of them. The word consequence literally means an *occurring after* in the line of succession. It by-passes the question of whether or not the *occurring after* was the result of active causation.

In discussing "the relevance of the Biblical doctrine of grace to the experiences of life" Niebuhr says, "It would be wrong to look for validation of the Biblical doctrine in some natural experience of grace. If our analysis of the relation of faith to reason, and of the 'Holy Spirit' to the spirit of man be correct, the experience which validates the doctrine can only be prompted by the doctrine itself."[1] Since a doctrine is a belief held intellectually by the human mind, if a doctrine initiates the experience of grace in a man then the initiation of grace is initiated by human activity, not by the supernatural power of God breaking the creation barrier and coming to man's assistance. The fact that Niebuhr has put the words Holy Spirit in quotation marks corroborates this conclusion. All of this is completely in line with Niebuhr's definition of grace. "The experience of grace in religion," he says, "is the apprehension of the absolute from the perspective of the relative."[2] Professor Henry Nelson Wiemann points out that for Niebuhr God's grace to an individual "is equated with the psychological effects of holding certain beliefs."[3]

When a man confronts the Cross he "experiences the mercy and new life which *flows from true repentance*,"[4] rather than from the Almighty Creator God acting upon and within him.

---

[1] (2) HD. pp. 119f, 120a. The quotation marks around *Holy Spirit* are Niebuhr's, showing that he is using the expression only in a symbolic sense, and not in its traditional sense of the Third Person of the Trinity.

[2] REE. p. 218e. The word "absolute" is not capitalized.

[3] Henry Nelson Wieman, "A Religious Naturalist Looks at Reinhold Niebuhr," p. 347 in Charles W. Kegley, and Robert W. Bretall, editors, *Reinhold Niebuhr His Religious, Social, and Political Thought* (New York: The Macmillan Co., 1956).

[4] SDH. p. 98c. Italics mine.

In the occasion of the *experience* only man, not God, is active: "Since perfection is love, the *apprehension of perfection* is at once the means of seeing one's imperfection and the consoling assurance of grace which makes this realization bearable."[1] This is something very different from saying that man's apprehension of perfection is the occasion both of man's realization of his own imperfection, and of God's active giving to the man the consoling assurance of grace.

"The sinner must feel himself 'justified,' that is, he must feel that his imperfections are understood and sympathetically appreciated as well as challenged."[2] Not only does Niebuhr's putting the word *justified* in quotation marks mean that he is using the word in his redefined sense and not in its standard meaning, but there is also no described action on the part of God relative to the individual man. Niebuhr does not say that God challenges the man for that would imply an interpersonal relationship between God and the man. Man's confronting the Cross is a situation wholly within the intellectual and historical sphere in this world. It is the human spirit's apprehension of this historical event that challenges him. Because the perfection of the Cross is the supreme example of love Niebuhr and the Christian's experience he is describing are deducing that God is loving. Here again, the deduction as well as the scene that initiates the deduction are both completely within the creation. No assisting action of the supernatural God is involved. At this point Niebuhr and the Christian whose experience he is describing then deduce—again a process where only human action is involved—that God (since he has been previously deduced to be loving) can also be deduced to understand and sympathetically appreciate the human being's imperfections. Assuming these deductions to be correct, there is still no account of God's interpersonal relationship with the man. Earlier in this book I have used in regard to Deism

---

[1] REE. p. 285cd. Italics mine.
[2] REE. p. 285ab. The quotation marks are Niebuhr's.

the crude anachronistic figure of God watching the human scene by a celestial television that has total coverage. If we look at the implications of this analogy and think of ourselves as watching a live production of *Hamlet* on our own television sets, we realize at once that we would be "understanding" Hamlet's "imperfections" and difficulties and "sympathetically appreciating him" and them. But we also see that the action of "sympathetic appreciation" which follows our "understanding" is only action of our mind and spirit relative to the information within our mind. In no sense is the action of our "sympathetic appreciation" a thing that in any way assists, or is in any way an interpresonal relation with, the Hamlet in his tragic predicament whom we are watching. Thus the statement that God "understands" and "sympathetically appreciates" repentant sinners does not by itself say that God makes any effort to assist them or to enter into an interpersonal relationship with them.

"The holiness of God thus creates both the consciousness of sin and the consolation which makes the consciousness of sin bearable."[1] "The sinner is 'justified' even though his sin is not overcome."[2] Here again, there is no real breaking of the creation barrier. As usual, the word *justified* is not used in its standard theological meaning. Had Niebuhr said that *the holy God creates* he would have been saying that God's power creates both consciousness of sin and consolation. But "the holiness of God" is merely the description of a quality and so it is only an abstraction unless it is accompanied by living power. It needs always to be kept in mind that the *modus operandi* of this "holiness of God" always reduces itself in Niebuhr's thought to the following: Man sees that love is righteousness in its highest form. Man sees the highest expression of love that he knows in the crucifixion of Jesus. Man believes that the stream can-

---

[1] REE. p. 290e.
[2] REE. p. 281ef. Quotation marks Niebuhr's.

not rise higher than its source and so man deduces that God must be characterized by a love like Jesus' love. Since the death of Jesus is his outgoing love to men it is consoling. Since his death is also historical evidence that humanity would have to be characterized by evil to inflict so horrible a death upon so good a man, a serious confronting of Jesus' death in one's thinking brings one inescapably up against the fact of one's own sinfulness. If one honestly reorients one's life in line with this honest facing of Jesus' suffering and love and one's own sinfulness, one feels that one has put one's self in line with the character and wishes of God, and so one has rightly made life's basic adjustment, and one is at peace. In all this there is no breaking of the creation barrier whatever. All the knowledge and activity involved come from within the human situation. Niebuhr's own great personal devotional fervor and the closeness with which his use of words seems to follow the Orthodox pattern tend to make a person who is studying Niebuhr for the first time read into his writings more of the traditional structure of Christian belief than his writings really contain. For after the confrontation of the Cross the "new self" is only the old self with "the vicious circle of self-centeredness . . . broken. The self lives in and for others, in the general orientation of loyalty to, and love of, God."[1] But no divine power has been added to the human life to begin the transformation of it by the gradual actual eradication of sin and by strengthening it with the power of the Divine Life to fit the human being for the life to come.

Since the Cross according to Niebuhr is essentially tragic, the peace that results from confrontation of it is largely the serenity that comes from the acceptance of defeat:

> For wherever judgment defines the limits of human striving it creates the possibility of an humble accep-

---

[1] (2) HD. p. 110a.

tance of those limits. Within that humility mercy and peace find a lodging place.[1]

The contrite recognition of the imperfections of the self further reduces the strain of living in an imperfect world because it reduces the presumptions and demands which the soul makes upon the world and upon its fellow-men.[2]

This is a far cry from the radiant joy and hope and sense of victory already won by Christ that meets one with such quickening power throughout the New Testament that J.B. Phillips, as he tried to translate its original Greek into modern English, said that he "felt rather like an electrician rewiring an ancient house without being able to 'turn the mains off.' "[3]

In Niebuhr's description of the converted sinner's relation to God at the Cross we see a great effort to describe some real intercourse between God and the human spirit. But Niebuhr is unconvincing here as he was unconvincing when he tried to describe revelation. And the reason is the same in both cases: any real Divine human intercourse would involve a breaking of the creation barrier and Niebuhr's thought will not admit this as a possibility.

The idea of a person's entering at the point of repentance and conversion upon a life of deepening personal fellowship with God—traditionally described in Christianity as the work of the Holy Spirit in the believer's heart—cannot be accounted for in terms of Reinhold Niebuhr's theology. Professor Soper points out that this lack of description of the soul's fellowship with God is one of the standard criticisms of Niebuhr's theology. Soper says:

The attack from the right insists that Niebuhr overestimates forgiveness and underestimates fellowship; that he does not see that repentance, necessary though

---

[1] IAH. p. 64a.
[2] REE. pp. 283f, 284a.
[3] J. B. Phillips, *Letters to Young Churches* (New York: Macmillan, 1957), p. xi.

it is, is not the end but the means to the end. True, the broken heart is the only entrance to the Kingdom, not alone at the beginning of the Christian pilgrimage, but every day, and as much at the end as at the beginning. Yet the nature of the Kingdom is mutual love, between God and the soul, and between the soul and society; the agape fellowship is the end, forgiveness the means. Intentionally or not Niebuhr leaves you with the reverse impression.[1]

Strangely enough, Professor Soper does not seem to realize that the choice of impressions was not an optional one for Professor Niebuhr.

Love in the Christian sense is actively outgoing, not the static lack of disharmony. Because Niebuhr is unable to describe God as active in his relation to men he cannot substantiate his claim that God loves men. Niebuhr talks constantly about the crucifixion being the great evidence of God's love for man. What never seems to occur to him is that *if Jesus Christ was not actually incarnate Deity and if he did not actually rise from the dead, then Calvary is entirely man's gift to God.* If God showed no mercy to Jesus in regard to the crucifixion—by neglecting to raise him from the dead afterwards—how can Jesus' death be the visible pledge of the Invisible Mercy? It is at best a guarantee of an element of heroic love in the human make-up confronted by Divine Indifference. Niebuhr has crusaded against the monistic tendencies in Liberalism and favored a return to the Hebrew-Christian insistence that God is righteous. But the claim that God is righteous breaks down if he permanently left Jesus of Nazareth in the lurch on Good Friday.

For Niebuhr it is the Atonement that is significant in the career of Jesus.[2] The "Cross is the fulfillment."[3] "The

---

[1] David Wesley Soper, *Major Voices in American Theology.* (Philadelphia: The Westminster Press, 1953), p. 40.

[2] SDH. 91de.

[3] (2)HD. p. 6c.

perfect love which His life and death exemplify is defeated, rather than triumphant, in the actual course of history."[1] "The Kingdom of God enters the world on tragic terms."[2] Since "the perfect love of the life of Christ ends on the Cross,"[3] there is about "the Cross" a "tragic perfection."[4] "Most profoundly the atonement of Christ is a revelation of what life actually is."[5] Therefore in "Christian tragedy" the religious person is described as *achieving* a renewal of life through a contrite submission to destiny."[6]

Since Jesus of Nazareth was not God Incarnate but only a representative of Deity[7] it is hard to see how his human suffering could be the "revelation of God's own suffering"[8] except, using the theory that the stream cannot rise higher than its source, "the beauty of vicarious suffering in history" can be thought to reveal "the very character of the divine."[9] But if God never breaks the creation barrier it is hard to see how his suffering—as he watches intimately by celestial television the ongoing of the world —can be more than sorrowful regret for "sin's rebellion against goodness."[10] There is no explanation given of how his suffering could also be his "voluntary acceptance . . . of the consequences of sin,"[11] or how God could be "Himself the victim of man's sin and pride."[12]

Niebuhr describes God's ultimate strategy in dealing with sin by saying that God "takes the consequences of His wrath and judgment, upon and into Himself."[13] This

---

[1] FH. p. 135c.
[2] BT. p. 184bc.
[3] (1) HN. p. 164b.
[4] (2) HD. p. 81cd. And see BT. p. 155d.
[5] BT. p. 20cd.
[6] FH. p. 9ab. Italics mine.
[7] (2) HD. pp. 45a, 46a; FH. p. 141cd.
[8] FH. p. 142fg; (2) HD. pp. 55f, 56a.
[9] (1) HN. p. 143f; DST. p. 177a-d.
[10] (2) HD. p. 56a.
[11] (2) HD. p. 56a.
[12] (1) HN. p. 148a.
[13] (2) HD. p. 55f.

is straight Orthodox teaching, but in Orthodoxy the *modus operandi* of this strategy is explained by saying that this was effected by God actually becoming incarnate so that Jesus Christ was a historical figure who was literally the God-Man. Thus the death on Calvary is consistently described as God literally experiencing the consequences of his wrath and judgment. However for Niebuhr, Jesus of Nazareth is not incarnate Deity, but only the symbol of God's suffering love. This makes the death on Calvary entirely man's gift to God. When one delves deeply into Niebuhr's teaching one always finds his God strangely inactive. If Jesus Christ is not God as well as man, how it can be truly said that God's divine love "takes the evil of history into and upon itself" is even more problematical.[1] Niebuhr's formula is that "the good news of the gospel is that God takes the sinfulness of man into Himself."[2]

This formula when analysed proves to be most unhelpful. It looks as if it means something because Niebuhr is thinking in pictures and there is a physical analogy embedded in his formula. This physical analogy in its original meaning is quite comprehensible. It is the picture of something physical surrounding and swallowing up some other physical thing. For example, suppose a very little fire starts where no fire should be. A rug can quickly be thrown over it, and by surrounding smother it. Or suppose two very small boys are squabbling about which shall have a particular piece of candy. If a big boy then comes along and grabs and eats the piece of candy he is ending the quarrel by swallowing up and destroying the bone of contention. Niebuhr seems to have some such general idea in mind when he says that "God takes the sinfulness of man into Himself."

But a spiritual, non-physical thing cannot be destroyed by taking it into one's self. One lessens the potency of a

---

[1] FH. p. 125d.
[2] (1) HN. pp. 142d, 143a; (2) HD. p. 46b.

spiritual thing only by repudiating it. And sin is a spiritual thing. If we take music into ourselves we become more musical. If we take an education into ourselves we become learned. If we take love into our hearts we become loving. And if we take sin into ourselves we become sinful. In each case we increase the total amount of the thing by taking it into ourselves. But insofar as we avoid music, education, love, or sin the total amount of those things is lessened. This is a law of spiritual existence. Niebuhr can scarcely mean that God becomes sinful by taking sin into himself, but that would be what would happen if God took man's sinfulness into himself.

One must distinguish carefully between sinfulness and a sinful person. Sinfulness is all sinful, by definition. On the other hand a sinful person is a being who, as the creation of God, is valuable,[1] but who is dangerously tied up with and infected by sinfulness which is very bad. It is because this distinction can be made that it is possible to love the sinner while hating the sin. By taking a sinner into one's love it is possible to take him to some extent into one's self, while at the same time repudiating his sinfulness. To give an example of this: If a young man of high moral and cultural standards and strong character and a girl of lower moral and cultural standards fell very much in love with each other what might happen is that under the power of love the girl might morally and culturally improve. It would not follow that she had lost her bad qualities by her lover taking them into himself. In his love he would take her—as distinct from her evil qualities—into his love, and she, in responding to and reciprocating his love would then begin to acquire something of his good qualities. As she took on his good qualities they would displace from her life the undesirable qualities that had previously characterized her. The expulsive power of a great affection plays a strategic part in the spiritual life. To the extent to which she took on his good qualities her bad qualities would be lessened by avoidance.

---

[1] Genesis 1:31.

To say that a person while remaining good does not take the sinfulness of another into himself does not mean that a good person cannot take the physical or social consequences of another's sin into himself. This is vicarious suffering. God could take the physical and social consequences of men's sin into himself only by literally becoming incarnate. Orthodoxy believes in God's literal Incarnation as Jesus Christ but Reinhold Niebuhr denies it.

Where the spiritual identification with the other is very close it is possible for the vicarious suffering of the one who loves to involve a real burdening of his spirit with the sin of another. But even this would not be an instance of taking the sin of another into himself for a burden is something extraneous to one's self weighing unpleasantly upon one's self. Thus the parent of a delinquent son, who was waiting trial for burglary, might so identify himself with his child that he would suffer vicariously the feelings of fear, shame, and guilt that were appropriate to the situation of the young man. It is in some such fashion that Paul's extreme saying about Christ, that God "made him to be sin who knew no sin,"[1] must be understood.

In this illustration of the parent of the delinquent child we can assume for the sake of argument that the parent was not at fault in the way he had brought up his son. The feelings of fear, shame, and guilt that the parent would feel for his erring son would definitely not be a taking of the son's sinfulness into himself. For after the sinfully motivated theft had been committed the feelings of fear, shame, and guilt, all of which testify to the heinousness of the deed, are good; that is to say, they are under the circumstances morally appropriate feelings. They are a testimony to the majesty of outraged righteousness and are therefore the youth's first step toward admitting the authority of righteousness and so his first step toward repentance and reformation. The feelings of shame, fear, and guilt are a terrible

---

[1] II Corinthians 5:21.

good, for goodness can sometimes be terrible. In participating in the erring child's feelings of fear, shame, and guilt, or in the feelings of fear, shame, and guilt that the child ought to feel, the parent would be participating in a terrible good. If, instead of this vicarious suffering, the parent busies himself trying to get his son out of the difficulty by attempting to bribe a witness to give perjured testimony, *then* the father could be truly said to take the son's sinfulness into himself! For in this case the father would be acting in conformity to the sinful line of direction initiated by the son, and so by his own sinning would have taken sin into himself.

Even supposing Niebuhr's formula were accurate and God could take man's sinfulness into himself, what good does Niebuhr think would come of it? He explains this by another formula, which is that in the "crucifixion God has absorbed the contradictions of historic existence into Himself."[1] This formula also looks plausible and desirable until it is analysed. When it is analysed it is seen to be un-Christian. According to Christian teaching Christ by his crucifixion won single handed the strategic battle against the powers of evil in the universe. The peace that passeth understanding is guaranteed for his followers by this victory. This Christian peace is very different from Hinduism's great attempt to get peace by describing Deity as absorbing the contradictions of historic existence into Itself, and so reaching the harmony of an Allness which cancels out both good and evil by being indifferent to both. Niebuhr's formula, that in the "crucifixion God has absorbed the contradictions of historic existence into Himself," is far more in line with Hinduism than it is with Christianity. The crucifixion does of course make glaringly apparent that great sin, great evil of misfortune, and heroic righteous love can coexist in the totality of a single historical situation. But to say this is not the same as saying that Jesus absorbed

---

[1] BT. pp. 192f, 193a. See also BT. pp. 19d, 168b.

the contradictions of historic existence into himself. It is only to say that, since virtues are most apparent at the testing point, the willingness on the part of a person to repudiate sin and follow love at the price of undergoing extreme pain, identifies virtue and strengthens it in the life of the person who practices this heroic virtue, and that the suffering, by making the spiritual power and beauty and goodness of the virtue apparent to others, allures many by its spiritual authority, which is the authority of the Good.[1] Thus, once evil exists, it can be made use of by Goodness for its own purposes. Furthermore, even to say that Jesus' death does do this is not to say that God has done it in the crucifixion unless one assents to the claim that Jesus is literally Deity incarnate, and this Niebuhr steadily refuses to do.

It has seemed advisable to tear those two formulae of Niebuhr's apart in a good deal of detail because they are central to his teaching of the relation of God to man in the Atonement. The crucifixion occupies an important place in his religious thought, but when he tries to invest it with religious meaning while at the same time being unable to hold the belief in a genuine Incarnation and genuine Resurrection he is forced into a most unfortunate fuzziness of thinking. This is why one feels that one has been feeding upon wind when one goes to Niebuhr's writings for help in the religious life.

But granting for the sake of argument Niebuhr's theory of the Crucifixion we must now see what follows in the life of any individual who seriously recognizes the Crucifixion as the symbol of God's suffering love, and so repents. We can say at this point: *Here beginneth the Christian life*. We must now ask ourselves, what is the history of the Christian life from this point on? How does God carry on with rela-

---

[1] See *ante,* p. 9, the quotation from William Temple.

tion to the individual and how does the individual carry on with relation to God? In other words, what is the life lived in grace?

"The question," says Niebuhr, "is whether the grace of Christ is primarily a power of righteousness which so heals the sinful heart that henceforth it is able to fulfill the law of love; or whether it is primarily the assurance of divine mercy for a persistent sinfulness which man never overcomes completely."[1] The question of whether grace is primarily a power is of course the point upon which everything turns. For if grace is a power it is the direct action of the Holy Spirit of Deity, and this traditional interpretation of grace includes the belief that God is breaking the creation barrier to assist the daily life of the Christian. Since Niebuhr declines steadily to admit the miraculous he is forced to hedge on this issue by saying that "the idea of grace can be stated adequately only in mythical terms."[2] One does not have to take a myth literally,[3] so one would not, if taking grace mythically, have to admit that any power direct from the supernatural God enters the natural man. Niebuhr candidly admits that "every effort to state the idea of grace and forgiveness of God in purely rational terms suffers from the same difficulties encountered in stating the conception of the relation of God to the world."[4] The difficulties of course all hinge on the question made acute by science, of whether a supernatural God can break the creation barrier and directly bring about sporadic desired effects within his creation. While traditional Christian theology never claims that rational human thought can give an exhaustive description of the mystery of God's grace, it does claim that up to a point it can be rationally described. The sins, bewilderments, weaknesses, and pains that beset man are not mythological and they can be rationally described.

---

[1] CPP. p. 18c.
[2] REE. p. 290cd.
[3] CPP. pp. 183e-184a, 220f-221a.
[4] REE. p. 290c.

If grace is adequate to deal with these difficulties it must be a genuine something that can be rationally described and that is not mythological.

In Niebuhr's clearest statement of what he means by the experience of grace, which is initiated when man confronts the Cross, he says, "Since perfection is love, the apprehension of perfection is at once the means of seeing one's imperfection and the consoling assurance of grace which makes this realization bearable."[1] *"Essentially the experience of grace in religion is the apprehension of the absolute from the perspective of the relative."*[2] Significantly it is the human "contrition which appropriates the divine forgiveness" and the "divine mercy" and which "lays hold upon a power beyond himself which both completes his incompleteness and purges him of false and vain efforts at self-completion."[3] It is not God laying hold of the individual human being. The activity is on the human rather than on the divine side. The word "purges" in this context simply means "ends," and the expression "power beyond himself" does not capitalize "power" and so does not make unequivocably clear that it is God that the Christian lays hold on.

There are two factors in this lack of clarity. One is that one can lay hold on a power beyond one's self that is not God. If I inadvertently touch a live wire, or if I step on an escalator in a department store, or if I telephone the police department that a thief has stolen my auto, I am in each case laying hold on a power beyond myself. The other factor relates to the nature of power. Power characteristically responds if one lays hold on it: the live wire will give me a shock; the escalator will carry me up to the second floor; the police department will go into action to try to recover my car and arrest the thief. If on the other hand I pick up a piece of paper from the floor and throw it into the wastebasket, the action is entirely on my side.

[1] REE. p. 285cd.
[2] REE. p. 281e. Italics mine.
[3] (2)HD. pp. 56f, 57ab.

The paper as I pick it up does not exert power upon me. *My sight of the paper* recalls the *idea* that I do not like to see the floor littered, and *this idea of mine* governs my action in picking up the paper and throwing it away. But the piece of paper itself is a powerless entity and exerts no power upon me. The paper is by its nature static.[1] So even if Niebuhr were right in saying that it is man who lays hold on a power outside himself, instead of saying that the Power of the Supernatural Creator God lays hold upon a man, he still would not have made good his claim that what the man lays hold of outside of himself is a *power*. For if what the man laid hold on were really power and not merely an idea or not merely a static entity, the thing laid hold on would initiate action relative to the man: as the live wire initiates unpleasant electrical shock; the escalator carries me somewhere by a power that does not reside in my person; and the police department gives me social assistance that I would be helpless without.

A Christian reading the quotation from Niebuhr with the traditional Christian scheme of salvation in mind would assume that it is the actual Power of the living God to which he is referring. But that is the reader's assumption rather than Niebuhr's direct statement. Furthermore, whatever the power is, can the consequences of laying hold upon it be proved from Niebuhr's statement to be anything more than the experience of a man's seeing his appropriate place in subordination to God, which experience ends the man's feverish and futile attempts to preserve and make sense out of his own existence by subordinating the world to himself? One can know one's self subordinate to God in the scheme of existence without describing God in anything more than Deistic terms.

Even the following more Orthodox sounding passage in *Faith and History* may mean only that when men are con-

---

[1] I am not of course referring to the latent power in the atoms comprising the paper. I am referring to the aspect of the paper with which we are dealing in this particular situation.

fronted with the crucifixion their view of human existence is spiritually clarified, and their life increases its own power by a radical reorientation and integration of itself:

> Such a point in human history [as the crucifixion] can be regarded both as the beginning of a new age for all mankind and as a new beginning for every individual man who is 'called'[1] by it, because both the individual and the collective realities of human existence are fully disclosed in it. If apprehended at all they are so apprehended that the old self, which makes itself its own end, is destroyed and a new self is born. That is why a true revelation of the divine is never merely wisdom but also power.[2]

All that Niebuhr is referring to here is the spiritual authority of the *idea* of the Good, and he is saying that the idea of the Good is recognized as fascinating by inherent right. Without this belief one could not have either Judaism or Christianity. But with this idea alone one could only have the best of Greek thought. It is basic to Jewish-Christian belief that the highest Good is also the Creating and All Controlling Intelligent Power.

But significantly the *agape* of Christ, as referred to by Niebuhr in the last quotation, is not "new life" itself but only its "norm." And the new life itself is not something God transmits to men, it is something "men may have" if "they discern what they are and what God is in this focal point of God's self-disclosure."[3] Again, we have another example of Niebuhr's skill in giving the illusion that God has interacted with the lives of men, without Niebuhr's making any real admission that the creation barrier has been broken. "The self" dies "to its narrow self, that it may truly live."[4]

---

[1] Quotation marks Niebuhr's.
[2] FH. p. 144f.
[3] FH. p. 144e.
[4] SDH. p. 238b.

Certainly a good deal is made of the element of clarification that results from man's confrontation of Jesus, for "in the epic of this life and death the final mystery of the divine power which bears history is clarified; and, with that clarification, life and history are given their true meaning."[1] He does not claim that men would "escape the tragedy of self-destruction in which all human life is involved," but he says that "it would cease to be a tragedy, if fully understood."[2] The experience of confronting " 'the love of Christ' "[3] is "the revelation of a divine mercy which understands us in the inevitable contradiction in which even the most perfect life is involved."[4] Again one is haunted by the idea that in Niebuhr's writings the Divine is viewing us by celestial television, understanding us sympathetically, but never *doing* anything about us.

For unless Jesus Christ is Deity incarnate the crucifixion is merely man's costly gift to God. And unless God took Jesus to everlasting joy with himself after the crucifixion and takes us also because of our relation to Jesus Christ, and unless the divine power of the Holy Spirit is literally and miraculously at work in the lives of Christians preparing them for this future joyous existence, then the creation barrier is never broken and all the pre-suppositions of "the good news" of the Christian gospel are false. In Niebuhr's writings we do not see God's love in action, and *the nature of love involving as it does an outgoing helpfulness to the person beloved, it is a real question of whether or not God's relation toward man could be one of love without specific divine action on a man's behalf. Therefore is not a belief that God does break the creation barrier essential if we are going to continue to claim that God is a God of love? And is not the confidence that the Creator of the universe is at once all powerful and supremely loving the basic source of Christian joy?*

[1] (2)HD. p. 55d.
[2] BT. p. 224cd.
[3] Quotation marks Niebuhr's.
[4] SDH. p. 233d.

There is a logical tie-up between the strange joylessness that characterizes Niebuhr's writings and his inability to believe that God breaks the creation barrier. The advantages that accrue to men in Niebuhr's account of the experience of (mythical) grace are of a somewhat negative sort. They are release from fear,[1] consolation for frustration,[2] and an attitude of resignation.[3] All these advantages can also be found in Hinduism.

The consolation and release from fear which follow the confrontation of the Cross make it possible for man more fully to fulfill his true nature which involves loving others:

> The essence of human nature is also love, which is to say that for man, who is involved in the unities and harmonies of nature but who also transcends them in his freedom, there can be no principle of harmony short of the love in which free personality is united in freedom with other persons.[4]

Man's "apprehension of the divine love. . . . leads to the renewal of life from self-love to love."[5] This does not prevent the human being, however, from remaining "within the vicious circle of sinful self-glorification on every level of moral advance."[6] Nevertheless Christians "have found in God the centre of existence and through loyalty to Him have learned to relate themselves in terms of mutual service to their fellows."[7] This love of their neighbor "is fed and supported by viewing the soul of the fellowman from the absolute and transcendent perspective,"[8] rather than by the Vine's constant nourishment of the branches,[9] which is

---

[1] FH. p. 144ab; FH. p. 176b; SDH. p. 91ef.
[2] REE. pp. 279de, 280ab.
[3] ICE. p. 89bcd; BT. p. 224bc; FH. p. 149ef.
[4] (1) HN. pp. 146f, 147a.
[5] FH. pp. 233f, 234a.
[6] (1) HN. p. 142de.
[7] BT. p. 258b.
[8] MMIS. p. 58a.
[9] John 15:4.

the relationship of the actually risen Christ to his followers, which involves a breaking of the creation barrier.

There are shortsighted thinkers who claim, "be good and you will be successful—in this life." There are deeper, more pessimistic thinkers who claim that real goodness gets a raw deal in life. Jesus' teaching followed neither of these alternatives. He believed that love and obedience to God would meet with suffering here and now but he did not consider the suffering tragic or a defeat. He considered it part of the tremendous battle for the great victory in the life beyond this. When men are persecuted Jesus tells them to "rejoice and be glad" for their "reward is great in heaven."[1] And certainly the early Church believed that "Jesus the pioneer and perfecter of our faith . . . for the joy that was set before him endured the cross, despising the shame, and is seated at the right hand of the throne of God."[2] For Christianity suffering love is never tragic. For "love is of God, and he who loves is born of God and knows God. . . . for God is love."[3] Those who are loving will share Christ's joy beyond this life. We are accustomed to look down our intellectually sophisticated noses at "simple" people who like story books in which the "bad guys" are ultimately foiled and the "good guys" *all live happily ever after.*[4] We forget sometimes that no melodrama we can devise makes such staggering claims for the ultimate ousting of evil and for God's servants "living happily ever after" as does the New Testament. The human situation is either actually set in that framework or it is not. The basic claims of the New Testament are either actually correct or they are mistakenly false.

---

[1] Matthew 5:11,12.
[2] Hebrews 12:2.
[3] I John 4:7,8.
[4] Intellectually sophisticated people who do not go in for this type of "sentimental" literature read instead "realistic" detective stories in which life has a basic moral framework, the good detective brings the "bad guy" to justice, and presumably the nice young things live happily ever after with the fortune the "bad guy" was trying to get.

In contrast to the New Testament, love, for Niebuhr, is basically tragic: "The self-realization through love which is promised does not carry the guarantee of historical survival.[1] It makes historical survival more problematic."[2] "Nations, as well as individuals, may be destroyed not only by violating the laws of life, but also by achieving a defenseless purity, incompatible with the necessities of survival."[3] "It is not a world of pure unity and the imperative of love leads to the destruction of the self as well as to its higher fulfillment."[4] "Thus the will to live is finally transmuted into its opposite in the sense that only in self-giving can the self be fulfilled."[5]

Niebuhr's belief that "individuals may be destroyed . . . by achieving a defenseless purity," and that a defenseless purity is "incompatible with the necessities of survival"[6] is inconsistent with his claim that God is good. Everyone knows that often saintly people like Jesus and St. Paul die martyrs' deaths. But, since many religions believe in some sort of personal existence beyond the grave, the word *killed*, when used theologically, is a word merely describing the event of death, while the word *destroyed* interprets this event as utter and final dissolution. For example, we say that Buddha taught his followers a regime leading to complete desirelessness, in order that the personality, after undergoing the painful vicissitudes of many *deaths* and many reincarnations, may at last be completely *destroyed*. There is no problem in Buddha's teaching in saying that when the personality becomes pure by desirelessness the personality is destroyed; for he desired the destruction of personality,

---

[1] And Niebuhr has no optimistic confidence in any other form of a person's survival as a person.

[2] FH. p. 197e.

[3] FH. p. 128b.

[4] ICE. p. 54c.

[5] CLCD. p. 19ef. See also BT. p. 155bc; FH. p. 149de; FH. p. 176bc; MMIS. p. 263de; (2)HD. pp. 45ef, 46a; (2)HD. pp. 74g, 75a.

[6] See above.

and there was in his teaching no good God whose relation to human life needed to be taken into account.

The word *God* includes the attribute of eternal being whether one is thinking of Brahman as the impersonal eternal ground of existence in the pantheistic sense or of Yahweh as the supernatural Creator. If God is Brahman no theological difficulty is involved if it is said that a human life that is characterized by the purity of a high degree of righteousness and love is hastening its own destruction. This is because righteousness and love are not characteristic of deity: the impersonal Brahman as the pantheistic ground of all existence includes righteousness and love indiscriminately with its inclusion of unrighteousness and hate, and so is actually indifferent to all good and evil.

But as soon as one makes the Jewish-Christian claim that the Eternal is characterized by the purity of righteousness and love one is describing an exclusive God: one is saying that he sides with love and righteousness against hate and unrighteousness. Since this God must necessarily be a personality if he is righteous and loving, and since he is by definition the Eternal, the characteristics of righteousness and love must be indissolubly tied up with his eternity, that is, with his characteristics of power and imperishability. *It would inevitably follow, therefore, that to the extent to which a human being increased in the purity of righteousness and love* (and even those who claim that basically all men are sinners agree that there is a somewhat closer approximation to goodness in a Florence Nightingale than in a Hitler) *he would be increasing in qualities more closely allied to the imperishable power of God than are the qualities of impure unrighteousness and hate which he is in the process of discarding. If God is pure, purity has to be compatible with survival and impurity with some form of destruction.* Therefore, for Niebuhr to hold that an individual's great increase in purity assists in his *destruction* denies the goodness of God, for it implies that the purity of righteous love is less closely linked to the imperishable power of God than is its opposite.[1]

Here is another way of stating the moral confusion to which Niebuhr's teaching leads: *If a human life is destroyed by achieving a defenseless purity then the undergoing of the crucifixion, by stripping from Jesus the God-like characteristics of living power and living personality, made Jesus less rather than more Godlike. And you, earnest, struggling, conscientious reader, by possessing at present a little fragile living personality and power, are at this moment more Godlike than Jesus is now.* For you, being alive, have a very small portion of power, even though that power is insecure and brief; and power is a characteristic of the Creator. And sinful though you are, your strenuous attempts to do what is right are relatively closer to the purity of righteous love than are the lives of such unmitigated scoundrels as the Duke in Browning's poem, "My Last Duchess." And righteous love is a characteristic of the Creator. You therefore are more Godlike than Jesus is at the present time, for Jesus, as *destroyed* on account of his great purity, now does not have life (which as life is to some extent Godlike); and as not having life he no longer has power (which as power is to some extent Godlike); and as lacking both life and power he no longer has now the purity of righteous love, for to be righteously-loving requires the exercise of choice, and without being alive and having some power, choice cannot be exercised. The so-called influence of Jesus in the twentieth century is not *his* power now, but only the power of *our* traditional and literary memory of him. So although Jesus *when he was alive* was more Godlike than you are now, and

---

[1] The idea that states which become too defencelessly pure hasten their own destruction does not pose the same theological problem. For it can be argued that if God is righteously loving his great interest is in individuals, because righteousness and love are interpersonal relationships. So if the individuals are preserved in a life beyond death the fact that nations perish is not a matter of ultimate concern. The idea of love being primarily for individuals rather than for man in the mass has been discussed at length, *ante* Chapter IV, pp. 60-68.

after you are dead *will have been* more Godlike than you *will have been,* nevertheless *at the present moment* you are *now* more Godlike than Jesus *is now*: A living dog is better than a dead lion.

The ancient Hebrews, who believed only in Sheol, used to insist that God would prolong the earthly days of the righteous and grant them worldly success. And they reiterated this claim at times when there must have seemed a great deal of evidence to the contrary. We err if we think them naive or materialistically crude about the religious life and the nature of God's rewards. They believed Yahweh to be the living God, and the powerful God, the righteous God, and the caring God; and they believed that He had created man in his own image and demanded that men try to live up to this image by trying to live righteous lives. If a man did his part by being righteous, the concomitant characteristics of God, power and prolonged life, ought to apply to God's servants also, if it is really true that God wants to have man in God's image. Jesus is strictly in line with this Old Testament insight. He only tells his followers to expect persecution and martyrdom and to take up their cross, because he has a vivid belief that their reward is great in heaven.[1] And early Christians believed that Jesus himself had "endured the cross, despising the shame" "for the joy that was set before him."[2] Over the centuries the ever subtler Hebrew insight into the inner nature of sin, which culminated in the harassed soul of the young Saul of Tarsus, was an attempt to guarantee the accuracy of the Hebrew faith that the Creator is righteous and has made man in his own image, even if more and more the burden of a recognition of human sin had to be laid upon men in order to justify the amount of human misery in the world, if the omnipotent Creator is righteous and cares for men. In the question of the relation of God to man the

---

[1] Matthew 5:11, 12.
[2] Hebrews 12:2.

165

early, shameful, and agonizing death of the completely innocent, unswervingly loyal Jesus was the exception that proves—in the sense of tests—the rule.

Niebuhr declares that "perfect detachment and perfect love are incompatible,"[1] and yet he has a curious emphasis on what he considers the virtue of "disinterestedness," although admittedly as he uses the word he is trying to emphasize the element in it of impartiality, not the element of apathy.[2] But if impartiality is all that he means he should have said "impartiality," for the word "disinterestedness" inevitably carries with it the sense of detachment and lack of interest that are more characteristic of the defeatist religions of the East than they are of the robust Christian love and hope. Disinterestedness in the sense of apathetic detachment is distinctly not a Christian virtue. Niebuhr's long discussion of disinterestedness comes in an early book, *Reflections at the End of an Era,*[3] and here at points the tie-up seems to be close between the virtue of disinterestedness and a spiritual defeatism.[4] In *Moral Man and Immoral Society* he says that "the religious ideal ... makes disinterestedness an absolute ideal without reference to social consequences."[5] In *An Interpretation of Christian Ethics* he speaks of "the complete disinterestedness which the ethic of Jesus demands."[6] And even in *Human Destiny* he speaks of Christ's "disinterested and sacrificial *agape,*"[7] which is the

---

[1] DST. p. 184b.

[2] REE. pp. 266a-f, 268a-e, 269c-e.

[3] See REE. pp. 266-280 especially.

[4] REE. pp. 279d-280b.

[5] MMIS. p. 263a.

[6] ICE. p. 31d.

[7] (2)HD. p. 71c. A most inept word with relation to Christ. Christian teaching through the centuries has taught that as there is in each human being the type of sin that helped crucify Christ, so Christ died for the sins of each separate person; and that Christ's love for each individual was so great that he would have gone through the crucifixion for the salvation of any single soul had that been necessary. If I seek Christ and am told that his attitude toward me is one of "disinterestedness" I have an emotional feeling of being rebuffed, because the emotional overtone of the word suggests that he lacks interest in me. If I were told that he loves me personally with

166

counterpart in history of "the perfect disinterestedness of the divine love."[1] The word used with relation to God creates a sense of chill in conjunction with Niebuhr's complete lack of indication that the heavenly Father did anything to help Jesus with respect to the crucifixion. A God who after Good Friday merely left the personal career of Jesus of Nazareth with a tragic ending and did not raise him as an individual person from the dead is a God whose "disinterestedness" is grim, to say the least, from the human point of view.[2]

As might be expected from our analysis so far, Niebuhr is fond of clinging to Biblical terminology, but he so redefines the well known terms that he robs them of their original New Testament meaning. This can be seen especially with reference to such specifically New Testament conceptions as Christ the Second Adam, resurrection, Christ at God's right hand, Christ's relation to the end of history, and Christ as the Judge of history.[3]

Niebuhr's theory of Christ as the Second Adam is not Paul's belief that "as in Adam all die, so also in Christ shall all be made alive. . . . The last Adam became a life-giving spirit. . . . Just as we have borne the image of the man of dust, so we shall also bear the image of the man of heaven."[4] For Paul's teaching involves the belief that in some way Christ actually stamps our human life with the deathlessness of Deity, and that definitely involves a breaking of the creation barrier. For Niebuhr, Christ as the Second Adam merely means that the character evidenced by

---

the same "impartial" love that he has for every person in Russia, China, and Africa I would be happy and not rebuffed. For I would then have a small place within his perfect love, and that would be a cause for joy. If one were unhappy because one did not possess his love exclusively, one would merely be giving evidence that one was thinking more about himself than about Christ's love.

[1] (2)HD. p. 72a.
[2] And see also (2)HD. p. 72de.
[3] See Appendix B.
[4] I Corinthians 15:22,45,49.

Jesus of Nazareth is "regarded as the revelation of the true character of man;"[1] and "to say that the innocency of Adam before the fall can be restored only in terms of the perfection of Christ is" merely "to assert that life *can approach its original innocency only by aspiring to its unlimited end.*"[2] Nothing miraculous or even specifically Christian is involved in the last quotation, especially since "unlimited end" means end as *telos* and not everlasting life.

The concept of resurrection is likewise very dear to Niebuhr. But resurrection does not mean for him the miraculous conquest of the forces of natural dissolution as the initiation of God's great harvest of human lives gathered to an everlasting life of joyous fellowship with himself. For Niebuhr "resurrection" merely means that "whenever the vicissitudes from which the self, either individually or collectively, suffers are appropriated by faith as divine judgments and not as meaningless caprice, they result in the love, joy, and peace of a new life."[3] It should be noted that this definition would mean that no people in the world have ever experienced "resurrection" as joyously and peacefully as the Hebrew people did before the coming of Christ, for no people before or since have ever so willingly interpreted their individual and collective suffering as deserved divine judgments. So according to this definition of resurrection the life of Jesus of Nazareth was not necessary as a prerequisite to people's "resurrection." It does not occur to Niebuhr to make this deduction from his own teaching. "Resurrection" as Niebuhr has defined it is the joyful, peaceful, loving spiritual consequences on earth only of the ap-

---

[1] (1) HN. 146e.
[2] (2) HD. p. 77c. Italics Niebuhr's. "Unlimited end" means end as *telos* and not everlasting life. Compare: "All things in history move towards both fulfillment and dissolution, towards the fuller embodiment of their essential character and towards death. The problem is that the end as *finis* is a threat to the end as *telos*. Life is in peril of meaningless because *finis* is a seemingly abrupt and capricious termination of the development of life before it has reached its true end or *telos*." (2) HD. p. 287bc.
[3] CRPP. p. 203b.

propriate orientation of one's life. But we have seen that he does not believe that the person of Jesus of Nazareth literally rose from the dead. Therefore Niebuhr's claim that the acceptance of the vicissitudes of the self as divine judgments has as a result the subjective experience of "love, joy, and peace of a new life" is a very shallow interpretation of the human predicament, inasmuch as this "resurrection" which Niebuhr is describing is limited to this life only. For on this interpretation, however much *we* may experience "resurrection" due to the true insight into the nature of existence afforded us by Jesus' death, Jesus himself never experienced "resurrection" on this interpretation of Niebuhr's. For Jesus' acceptance of the vicissitudes from which the self suffers issued not in the "love, joy, and peace of a new life" for him, but in the cry of dereliction on the cross. There was no time after that to experience joy and peace: he was dead.

It is doubtful whether, without a belief in the real Resurrection of Christ as the New Testament believed in it, it is possible for a person to find spiritual peace through a contemplation of the Cross. Certainly the twentieth century, made shy by science about admitting that the Early Church's belief about the Resurrection could correspond to actual fact, is a century that has tried by all devices possible to look away from the Cross. Even Reinhold Niebuhr himself does not look directly at the Cross, but only at a doctrine about it. Try really meditating upon the loving and sinless Jesus of the Galilean ministry undergoing crucifixion as realistically described by a modern writer:

> Our generation has never seen a man crucified except in sugary religious art; but it was not a sweet sight, and few of us would dare to have a real picture of a crucifixion on our bedroom walls. A crucified slave beside the Roman road screamed until his voice died and then hung, a filthy, festering clot of flies, sometimes for days—a living man whose hands and

feet were swollen masses of gangrenous meat. That is what our Lord took upon himself . . .[1]

If one believes that Jesus is not God Incarnate who rose triumphantly from the dead on Easter day, but instead believes that Jesus is merely a loving man to whose personal existence Good Friday wrote *finis,* can one really draw an experience of "love, joy, and peace of a new life" from the experience of confronting the Cross, without laying one's self open to the charge of sadism? How about drawing peace, if the victim of the crucifixion were your son or daughter?

Niebuhr's whole type of thought of course rules out a literal belief that Jesus Christ is now at the right hand of God.[2] For Niebuhr it is only in "a realm of meaning" that "the crucified Saviour is alive and 'sitteth at the right hand of God.' "[3] In other words the self-sacrificing goodness in the abstract of Jesus of Nazareth is now dear to God in a way that does not involve the actual person who lived on earth as Jesus of Nazareth having at present any conscious existence at all. For this type of thought holds that the world *and God* permanently faded from the consciousness of Jesus of Nazareth after he cried out, "My God, my God, why hast thou forsaken me?"[4] And it holds that, for the more than nineteen hundred years since that moment, Jesus of Nazareth has never once thought of God, because he has no consciousness with which to think.

The idea of Jesus Christ as the Son of Man passing judgment at the end of history, as described in the sheep and goats parable in Matthew,[5] would therefore of course be out of the question for Niebuhr. His conception of "Christ

---

[1] Joy Davidman, *Smoke on the Mountain* (Philadelphia: The Westminster Press, 1954), p. 20.
[2] For Niebuhr the crucifixion is a "tragic drama." FH. p. 144b.
[3] SDH. p. 237bc. Quotation marks Niebuhr's.
[4] Mark 15:34.
[5] Matthew 25:31-46.

as judge" is reduced to mean merely that "when the historical confronts the eternal it is judged by its own ideal possibility, and not by the contrast between the finite and the eternal character of God."[1]

Jesus of Nazareth does not play a part in the future end of history. It is the "Christ event" which is the "end" of history not as "finis" but merely as " *telos* " or purpose and goal.[2] This is just another way of saying that in the sacrificial life and death of Jesus we see a revelation of men's true nature which they ought to strive to attain.[3]

And yet Niebuhr sees "a peril in this" watered down "way of interpreting the Gospel truth. . . . We say we take historical facts seriously but not literally;" (and this would include the fact that the Gospels say one thing and not another) "but that may be on the way to not taking them as historical facts at all."[4]

We agree. Basic to the whole New Testament is the claim that Deity literally, and this means miraculously, entered into his creation to draw men to the joy of everlasting fellowship with himself, beyond sin and beyond the hazard of the decay of nature. Remove miracle from the New Testament and the thread is lost upon which the pearls of all the separate teachings are strung.

---

[1] (2) HD. 291e, 292a.
[2] SDH. p. 91bde.
[3] *Ante,* Christ the Second Adam.
[4] CRPP. p. 198ef.

CHAPTER VII

WHAT OF THE FUTURE

IT SHOULD BE SQUARELY faced that the question of the breaking of the creation barrier is the basic problem confronting modern theology. Honestly face the implications of giving up this belief and you will see that you have given up Christianity. If you do not think this situation is serious try to count on your fingers the number of religious leaders that you know who would be willing to give a straightforward answer in print, signed, to the following question: *How do you think of intercessory prayer as being valid, not just as a method of alerting the person who prays to take practical steps to assist others, or as a means of impressing others if they know they are being prayed for, but also as of genuine use in assisting God's direct divine assistance to come to others?* In six years of graduate study in three divinity schools and fifty years of regular church going I have never heard this question discussed. And yet intercessory prayer is essential to Christianity: it is embedded in the Lord's Prayer, which is a prayer for others as well as for one's self.

Without the breaking of the creation barrier a righteous (and therefore supernatural) God could not engage in active relatedness to individual men in their individual needs. Reinhold Niebuhr has made an all-out attempt to by-pass miracle and still keep Biblical Christianity and Niebuhr has failed. The inadequacy in his theology that has resulted from his repudiation of miracle has been felt by many critics who would hesitate to state the case for a miraculous Christianity as baldly as this book has stated it. The following examples are an indication of this uneasiness in regard to Reinhold Niebuhr's theology:

> On the other hand, does one not have a right to expect of every thinking Christian—and *a fortiori* of every Christian thinker—that he be cognizant of what he has to hope for in Christ? To what extent there stands behind Niebuhr's 'eschatological symbols' a *reality,* and what kind of reality—or whether perhaps these eschatological symbols are merely 'regulative principles' in the Kantian sense—these are questions on which we should like to have him make a definitive pronouncement.[1]

> Much of the Biblical narrative involves the miraculous, and it is not clear what is Niebuhr's final attitude toward miracle. On this matter his apologetic appears to falter. . . . Niebuhr is tempted to believe (with Bultmann) that there is much to be gained by dissociating the historical basis of Christian faith from any divine miraculous interventions in the realm of natural causation (for example, the Virgin Birth or the physical Resurrection). . . . He seems to suppose that Christian scholars who preach the gospel to ordinary people must necessarily practice some doctrine of reserve, 'as deceivers and yet true'; they must preach as history what they know to be merely symbolical. . . .

> There is nothing in Niebuhr's own analysis—at least as one reader understands it—to account for the hesitation and (to speak plainly) equivocation which appear in so much of his writing upon the historicity of the Gospel.[2]

> The Cross, which is apprehended and interpreted as the *basis* of a new wisdom and power, is not adequately apprehended and interpreted as *operative* wis-

---

[1] Charles W. Kegley and Robert W. Bretall, Editors, *Reinhold Niebuhr His Religious, Social and Political Thought* (New York: The Macmillan Company, 1956), p. 32. Emil Brunner, "Some Remarks on Reinhold Niebuhr's Work as a Christian Thinker."

[2] *Ibid.* pp. 225-227. Alan Richardson, "Reinhold Niebuhr as Apologist."

dom and power. The case is persuasively made for the content of the mythical apprehensions of faith symbolized in and by the Cross and for the way in which these apprehensions resolve the problem of the self and of historical existence. But the power by which this wisdom and power effectually works is less persuasively set forth, indeed, almost not at all.[1]

Besides this alleged power of belief to transform human life, there is God's grace. But when we examine Niebuhr's statements about God's grace we find that grace is equated (1) with the psychological effects of holding certain beliefs, and (2) with 'the provisional coincidence between the interests of a ruling group within a nation and the interests of the total community, or [with] coincidence between the interests of a powerful imperial community and the wider community of nations.'

Even Christ in us is not an actual power but only a hope, and therefore can operate only by way of the psychlogical effects of belief. 'Christ in us is not a possession but a hope.' (The Nature and Destiny of Man II, 125)[2]

The presupposition of his emphasis on justification by faith is his belief in the revelation of God in Christ, though his Christology is never fully elaborated. Niebuhr has little patience with metaphysical theories concerning the incarnation.[3]

The attempt Reinhold Niebuhr has made to by-pass miracle and still keep Biblical Christianity is so brilliant, sustained, and devout that I believe he has closed off a blind alley: if *he* cannot describe Biblical Christianity in non-miraculous terms then it cannot be so described. We are reduced to two alternatives. We can subscribe to some form of Pantheism—such as Hindu philosophy or Stoicism in

---

[1] *Ibid.*, pp. 277, 278. Paul Lehmann, "The Christology of Reinhold Niebuhr."

[2] *Ibid.*, p. 347. Henry Nelson Wieman, "A Religious Naturalist Looks at Reinhold Niebuhr."

[3] *Ibid.*, p. 48. John C. Bennett, "Reinhold Niebuhr's Social Ethics."

one of their modern "scientific" forms—and admit that we are discarding the Jewish-Christian religion as untrue. Or we can believe that the Jewish-Christian religion is true on the strength of the logic of righteousness, and then make an all-out intellectual attempt to work out a philosophy and theology that will include the advances of modern scientific thought and the Biblical description of the righteous supernatural creator God, who can break the creation barrier to reveal himself to men, to become incarnate and rise from the dead to make possible man's salvation, and to assist his followers by guiding, strengthening, and illumining their lives upon earth and by taking them to joyous companionship with himself in heaven after they have died.

The basic inconsistency that unhinges the whole theology of Reinhold Niebuhr relates to miracle. He had seen in his early years at Detroit that the monistic or pantheistic theologies undergirding Liberalism hamstrung Liberalism's ability to say a prophetic word about the righteousness of God and the sin of man, which was a message sorely needed by a complacent but endangered Western civilization. To speak the prophetic message he was forced to deny the monistic theologies and describe God as transcendent. His line of argument is that the Jewish-Christian religion is a religion of revelation in which God reveals himself to man in his mighty acts, culminating in Christ's Atonement. The self-sufficiency of the manmade religions is an indication of the basic sin of pride, which is a rebellion against the Creator in refusing to admit one's position as creature before him, and attempting instead to make one's self the center of one's universe and the ultimate source of one's safety.

But because Niebuhr is unable to describe God as breaking the creation barrier to reveal himself in Old Testament times, the specific content of the Old Testament religion is reduced to man's deduction from naturally caused events in history. And because Niebuhr cannot think of God as breaking the creation barrier to genuinely incarnate himself as Jesus Christ, Calvary becomes entirely man's gift to God, and so the specifically Christian revelation turns out to be man made. So Niebuhr has not genuinely established the Jewish-Christian tradition as a religion of revelation.

Furthermore, by not admitting the breaking of the creation barrier Niebuhr cannot admit any assistance offered to Jesus himself by God after the ninth hour on Good Friday. This raises the question of whether God is, as a matter of fact, trustworthy. Because if God at this point left Jesus in the lurch, what right have we to think that God is righteous and loving and that he respects and cherishes *our* human personalities? But if God is not righteous and loving and if he does not cherish human personality, then man has really been abandoned by God to be on his own. So Niebuhr's whole case for the heinousness of man's sinfulness breaks down, because by his argument man is convicted as a sinner for not trusting God, but instead for trying to organize the world around himself, in order to make his own strength the source of his security. But a man could be sinful in making himself the source of his own security only if in so doing he was spurning the proffered love and assistance of a righteous God. However, if God does not actually act in a lovingly assisting way toward men, then God has in fact abandoned men to find what security they can for themselves on their own. Either that, or else God wants men to be insecure, having no security on their own and no security through him. If that is the case, then God cannot be described as loving men. In fact, since we think of human beings who delight in making others insecure as fiendish, the kindest thing that one could say about God would be that he is lacking in righteousness.

It is simply not fair to claim that Jesus' promise that "Whoever loses his life for my sake will find it"[1] is fulfilled if the dying martyr, in the last few agonizing seconds before he permanently perishes, realizes that he has done

---

[1] Matthew 16:25.

the right thing. The first martyr, Stephen, when he died, obviously expected more from Jesus' promise than that. Just before Stephen died he said, "Behold, I see the heavens opened, and the Son of man standing at the right hand of God." And as Stephen was dying he said, "Lord Jesus, receive my spirit."[1] On Niebuhr's belief Jesus was not at that moment at the right hand of God because God had not cared enough for him at Calvary to perpetuate his individual existence. And so there was at that time no living Jesus to know Stephen's predicament and rescue him to fellowship beyond death with God.

To claim that a man is sinful if he looks for a security apart from God, when God is known to be so callously indifferent to men that he regularly sells his martyred servants down the river, is to outrage our sense of ethical decency. The inability to believe that Jesus as a person actually rose from the dead (which would involve breaking the creation barrier) undercuts, therefore, the force of Niebuhr's ethical message when he inveighs against man's sinfulness.[2]

This is not to discount the personal impressiveness of Niebuhr as a man in the role of a prophet. He, like the prophets of the Old Testament, has steadily insisted on God's righteousness in the face of impending national disaster and the personal disaster of death, without the encouragement of belief in divine help beyond the grave. Among the nations of the world only Israel has had the devotion to God and the strength to do this steadily. And the greatness of Israel's devotion has helped make it possible for God to use this nation to teach the world.

It is true that a man ought to trust and obey God even without hope of reward as far as his own life is concerned. And God has so devised it that the iron curtain of death acts as a screening process in that regard, for it forces all men sometimes to choose the alternative immediately dis-

[1] Acts 7:56,59.
[2] See *ante* pp. 70-72.

advantageous to themselves, when they are not sure of the outcome in this life or really assured (emotionally) of a life to come, so that they are forced to gamble their safety on a blind clinging to righteousness. What most earnest Christians do at some point in their lives Israel—and Reinhold Niebuhr—have done steadily. And the evidential importance of their witness cannot be overestimated.

But in addition to a theologian's personal religious devotion there is also the reasoned statement of his faith, and in this regard we are Christians and not Jews, and so we must take the life and death of Jesus into consideration. Even Jewish thought which believed at first that justice was done if God rewarded and punished the nation (Amos), came to see that if God is righteous he must be interested in the individual (Jeremiah), and then that God if he is righteous must punish and reward the individual (Ezekiel). Then in the second century B.C. (in the book of Daniel) the problem of how God can reward his martyred servants turned Jewish thought to a belief in a life after death. The problem that raised the issue of life after death for the book of Daniel is raised in such an acute form for Christians by the death of Jesus that Christians are forced to see the righteous character of God himself as at stake in the Resurrecion.

Reinhold Niebuhr's theory that the suffering of the righteous Jesus—the "tragedy" of Calvary—is evidence that there is suffering in the heart of the Creator is insufficient as the final picture of God, for if suffering is the ultimate picture of Deity, it implies that the Creator is really defeated by the sin of men. Niebuhr nowhere gets to a vivid description of joy in the heart of God, and in his writings the sense of beauty is almost completely lacking. One would expect anyone with as Hebraic a point of view as Niebuhr has not to develop his theological argument along the line of the implied logic of aesthetics,[1] be-

---

[1] William Temple uses the lines of direction of the logic of love, ethics, and art to substantiate his apology for Christianity.

cause the Bible avoids claiming that beauty is a road to God. The Bible austerely avoids dependence upon beauty because the desire to surround one's self with what is physically beautiful may make one spiritually shortsighted and foster ethical callousness. But the beauty of nature is morally safe because it is a beauty accessible equally to rich and poor. The appreciation that the Old Testament shows of the beauty of nature as transfigured by the glory of its Creator has never been surpassed in literature and the Old Testament idea of "the glory of God" contains the ingredient of superlative beauty. The psalmist wished "To behold the beauty of the Lord, and to inquire in his temple."[1] The sense of beauty in the Old Testament is intense although it is austere, and for most twentieth century Americans an acquired taste.

On this point I can give the testimony of personal experience. Shortly after my undergraduate days, in distress at the spiritual aridity of Biblical criticism, I turned from the Bible and the clutter of theories that surrounded my knowledge of it to steep myself in the works of the great English poets. In their company I regained my spiritual equilibrium and sense of proportion and my confidence that value is a valid line of direction to follow in the search for Ultimate Reality. After a few years of this digression I gladly turned to the Bible and theology and for nearly twenty years I gave up the reading of poetry. A few years ago I decided to reread the great poems that had once meant so much to me and I was surprised to discover how thin and pale they seemed after the richer diet of the Old Testament to which I had become accustomed.

The reason that the Bible, although austere, is illumined by beauty and joy is that if God is God and the righteous Creator, then power, righteousness, love, success, peace, and the joy that is beyond (i.e., on the far side of) pain must coincide in the heart of God and be eventually shared by

---

[1] Psalm 27:4.

those who are united to God in a relationship of mutual love. If we were left with suffering as the ultimate picture of Deity as Niebuhr leaves us, then the Creator would be permanently defeated by the sin of men. But if God can be finally defeated by man he is not the all powerful righteous Creator. Conversely if God is the all powerful righteous Creator then righteousness and peace must eventually kiss each other. If one believes that a well intentioned God created the world which then became a kind of Frankenstein's monster that got out from under his control so that God himself is finally characterized by the pain of defeat and tragedy, then one has parted company with the whole tenor of Biblical religion. The absence of a sense of beauty and joy in Niebuhr's writings is especially conspicuous, because his whole theology has been an attempt to return to Biblical religion and make it applicable to twentieth century needs.

One of the reasons why the basic deviation of Niebuhr's thinking from Biblical faith is not more obvious than it is is that in his earnest desire to be intellectually of the twentieth century and at he same time to return to Biblical religion he has constantly tried to harmonize these two aspects of his thought by using Biblical terminology and quotations which he has redefined and reinterpreted to suit his own truncated form of Christian belief.[1] He keeps the old terminology on the ground that no one can ever fully describe God and the things of God, so that in speaking religiously one must always speak symbolically. This means that in conveying religious truth one has to some degree to falsify it.

It is true that it is presumptuous to assume that we know all there is to know about God, but if we believe the revelation of God through the Old Testament prophets, Christ, and Paul to be valid, then we have to believe that the *line of direction* of the truth about God and his relation to man is very firmly established. It is therefore permissible to

---

[1] See Appendix B.

speak symbolically about God and human destiny if we bear in mind that there are legitimate and illegitimate ways to use symbols.

For example: There was once a three year old girl who complained one morning as her father was leaving the house, "I don't want you to go away, Daddy; I want you to stay and play with me." He replied, "Daddy has to go to the office every day to get you and Mamma bread and butter." The next week the child's mother had her down town and took her to her father's office. The youngster rushed into his arms exclaiming, "I want some bread and butter." Since a three year old child cannot understand the intricacies of twentieth century finance the father's description of his daily absences from home as "getting her and her mamma bread and butter" had been honest legitimate symbolism even if the child somewhat misconstrued it. This is the sense in which it is ethical to be "as deceivers, yet true." This is because what the father was doing at the office was caring for the child's welfare in a far more adequate way than could be achieved by merely procuring slices of bread and butter for her. On the other hand, if in answer to her original objection to his leaving the house in the morning he had said, "I have to go to get you and Mamma bread and butter," when what he was really planning to do that morning was to desert his family and elope with his secretary, then his answer would not have been legitimate symbolism, it would have been plain lying. *Symbolism in religion relative to the Christian hope cannot be legitimately used when its surface meaning, if taken literally, is basically more adequate and desirable from the point of view of permanent human welfare than is the actual fact which the statement "symbolizes."* I regret to say that I consider Reinhold Niebuhr's "symbolic" use of many standard Christian terms and expressions illegitimate.

It is only fair to say that one finds within Niebuhr's overwhelming torrent of words honest definitions of his debased verbal coinage.[1] The difficulty is that the standard meaning of the words and phrases and Bible verses is so thoroughly fixed in the Christian's mind that the words, woven into the texture of Niebuhr's argument, carry the impression of the traditional meaning even after one has discovered their new definitions. Niebuhr can thus appear to be far more a defender of traditional Christianity than he actually is, according to the beliefs to which he really subscribes.

This deception must not be thought of as an intentional misleading of the reader. There are few theological books that give the reader the impression of hearing the author think out loud to the extent to which Niebuhr's books do. He really loves Biblical religion and his use of its terminology is primarily an attempt to warm himself at its fires,[2] rather than an attempt to convey a message that he disbelieves. But the problem of relating Biblical religion to the scientific view point cannot be solved simply be a redefining of the ancient terms, and the element of confusion in Niebuhr's thought is a testimony to the genuine intellectual perplexity that besets twentieth century religious leaders. To some extent Niebuhr's complaint is justified when as a young man he said, "If in this civilization we cannot inherit the kingdom of God because we cannot be as little children, the fault, dear Brutus, is in our stars and not in ourselves."[3]

It is time, however, that the question be squarely raised as to whether the retaining of the Christian vocabulary in the pulpit, on the part of ministers who do not believe the essential presuppositions of the New Testament writers, does not involve falsehood. Making all allowances for the intellectual difficulties the Protestant clergy have faced, and for their desire to transmit as much as possible of the Christian heritage when the content of their own belief was extremely meager, nevertheless the time eventually comes

---

[1] See Appendix B.
[2] See Appendix C.
[3] LNTC. p. 133ef.

when a *double entendre* in religious vocabulary and in public reference to Biblical passages, which conveys one idea to the laity and a differing idea to the theologically initiated, becomes unethical duplicity. Even if one ignores the seriousness of this situation for the personal careers of the clergy when faced with the judgment of Christ, who of all sins denounced most vigorously the hypocrisy of the religious leaders of his day, still one must be aware both that this situation is estranging from the Church many of our most earnest young people of high intellectual ability, and that this whole state of affairs is particularly deplorable at a time when America is conscious of being threatened by pagan ideologies from without and by a general breakdown in national integrity from within.

In justification for their tactics ministers speaking among themselves claim that in the popular presentation they withhold their own actual beliefs with the intent of comforting people with the old expected message even if the clergyman himself does not believe it is true. This raises two questions. One is whether this practice does not reveal a skepticism deeper than the skepticism as to the truth of Christianity, the more basic skepticism of denying the validity of honesty and intellectual integrity themselves. The second question that can be raised is whether those who act on the assumption that it is permissible to comfort the bereaved, the aged, the suffering, and the tempted with kindly meant lies have not given up belief in the dignity of the individual. For to act on the assumption that one can continue a human relationship with another person that is not based on the foundation of a mutual loyalty to Truth is to treat that other with contempt by reducing his dignity to the status of an animal's. We fulfill our duty in our relationship with domestic animals when we act with their comfort in mind. In human relationships one does not practise lies toward an individual whom one reveres. Have not those who should be our spiritual leaders unintentionally led the way to that abandoning of "reverence for personality"

183

which we too easily assume is a fault exclusively located behind the Iron curtain?

We inveigh against the Russians as dishonest when they redefine "democracy" to mean "the Communist form of government," and then claim to emerging poverty-stricken lands that Communist countries are "People's Democracies." Why is that any more dishonest than it is if a Christian pastor, when a dying grandmother, searching for some spiritual encouragement, says to him, "Do you believe in life after death?" answers encouragingly, "I surely do believe in the Resurrection." And he does not add that he has previously among his fellow ministers redefined "resurrection" to mean "only the carryover of influence due to the Church's historical memory." This type of religious double talk, characteristic of much of the American pulpit either explicitly or implicitly for at least forty years, is morally every bit as bad as it was for a college professor to take part in a rigged television quiz program which he pretended was *bona fide*. It is equally immoral for a preacher who does not believe that Jesus Christ is still living as a powerful, active, conscious-and-self-conscious personal spirit to talk of "the Christian's confrontation of Christ," if the preacher does not make it perfectly clear to his congregation that all that that expression means is "the Christian's confrontation of his own knowledge of the Jesus who lived and perished as an individual person in the first century."

One knows that ministers are hard pressed themselves by religious perplexities. And as Niebuhr himself pointed out early in his career, "One can never be quite sure where pedagogical caution ends and dishonesty begins."[1] But the essential claims of the New Testament are either true or they are not true. They involve the claim that the supernatural Creator of the world is a personal God—one who can truthfully be described as "Our Father, who art in heaven"—and

---

[1] LNTC. p. 11c.

that this personal God can and does interact with the world at particular sporadic points in off-schedule ways to further his great purpose, which concerns the bringing of human beings into fellowship with himself, and to this end strengthening and purifying and guiding their lives in order that they may serve him upon earth and attain joyous fellowship with him in heaven. Specifically this involves the breaking of the creation barrier at least at the points of the Incarnation and the Resurrection of Christ, the transferring of Christians to heaven at death, and the action of the Holy Spirit in inspiring Old Testament prophecy and in regenerating, purifying, strengthening, and guiding Christians throughout the succeeding centuries of the Church.

We have designated these particular activities of God as instances of breaking the creation barrier simply because they are off-schedule activities of God, not the routines by which he regularly supports the ongoing of nature. From the point of view of science these off-schedule activities appear to be miracle, for science concerns itself solely with investigating the regular ongoing routines of nature, and so finds the idea of the unscheduled insertion into nature of any power from beyond nature an embarrassment.

If one shares the embarrassment to such an extent that one cannot believe that God does break the creation barrier, then one should frankly give up Christianity and frankly embrace Stoicism or some form of Indian Pantheism. If, on the other hand, one believes, as Reinhold Niebuhr did when he formulated his religious position, that the demands of righteousness are an extra-scientific clue to the nature of Ultimate Reality, then one should accept the Christian claims of the breaking of the creation barrier on the ground that they are what would logically be true if Righteous Loving Power were the heart of reality. (Reinhold Niebuhr refused to follow the logic of righteousness the whole way.)

If one accepts the logic of righteousness and love as a clue to the nature of Ultimate Reality, then one can accept the belief in the breaking of the creation barrier. However, this frankly means that one is keeping one's religious belief and one's scientific understanding to some extent in separate compartments and that this is an unfortunate necessity but a legitimate procedure until Christian theology can be reformulated so as to include science without selling Christianity short.

In other words the reformulation of Christian theology, taking into consideration the intellectual advances of modern science, has not yet been adequately done. Need that surprise us? It took four hundred years for Christian theologians ending with Augustine to complete the work of acclimatizing Greek insights to the Christian message. Greek intellectual culture was an alien ideology of static content whereas the content of scientific ideology has been expanding by leaps and bounds. And it is now only about three hundred years since seventeenth century science had advanced far enough to make acute the problem of the relation between scientific investigations and the Christian faith. The crux of the difficulty still lies in the question of the breaking of the creation barrier. It is a question to which those who are called to serve Christ with the mind, both scientists and clergy, should bend their energies, keeping firmly in mind the intellectually perplexing elements that cannot be lost in the new theological synthesis, without betraying the Christian faith.

APPENDIX A

QUOTATIONS RELEVANT TO MIRACLE IN AUGUSTINE AND WILLIAM TEMPLE

WITH THE EXCEPTION of the Creation itself and Christ's Resurrection the great essential miracles of Christianity—the Incarnation, the assistance the indwelling Holy Spirit gives individual lives, and God's transferring his servants at death to heavenly fellowship with himself—are unspectacular to our human perception. The two nature miracles that seem most essential to the Old Testament occur at the incident of the crossing of the Red Sea and at the Contest on Mt. Carmel. Even here, if miracle took place, the miracle itself would be unspectacular.

For the miracle at the Red Sea would involve deflecting the air currents so that the "strong east wind" would be in sufficient strength at the proper spot and at the proper time to lower the water and let Israel get across. But as far as Moses and Israel were concerned, the miraculous action took place "off stage" before they were aware of what was happening. What would have happened would have been that God, who was aware of the nature of the emergency before Moses and Israel were aware, had quietly reset the air currents. No one saw or knew how or when God did it. The miracle had taken place far from the spot where its usefulness was to function. By the time the wind reached the vital point on the Red Sea the natural air currents *had already adjusted to the miraculous intervention and were now functioning normally, lowering the water to the same degree to which they always lowered it when they blew with that velocity in that direction.*

The miracle at Carmel also took place behind scenes. For God saw to it that Elijah—who did not know that a prominent, wet, isolated object on high ground was an exceptionally good lightning conductor—did as a matter of fact wet thoroughly the altar and sacrifice with another end in view. And God had inspired Elijah to call for the contest at a time when the drought was nearing its end (with or without supernatural intervention as the case may be). So the electrically charged atmosphere was already present and God in the end had only to maneuver slightly to synchronize inanimate nature with the activity schedule of his servant in a split second timing. This synchronization involves miracle. But when Elijah and Israel and the prophets of Baal saw the spectacular bolt from the blue demolish the altar and the sacrifice what they saw was a natural occurrence. *The absorption of special divine influence on the part of Elijah and inanimate nature had already taken place. Now lightning was striking naturally as it would always strike if those particular physical conditions were exactly duplicated.*

The belief in miracle I am advocating in this book is one comparable to that described in the following quotations from Augustine's *Confessions* and William Temple's *Nature, Man and God*:

FROM SAINT AUGUSTINE

And how shall I call upon my God—my God and my Lord? For when I call on Him I ask Him to come into me. And what place is there in me into which my God can come—into which God can come, even He who made heaven and earth? Is there anything in me, O Lord my God, that can contain Thee? Do indeed the very heaven and the earth, which Thou hast made, and in which Thou hast made me, contain Thee? Or, as nothing could exist without Thee, doth whatever exists contain Thee? Why, then, do I ask Thee to come into me, since I indeed exist, and could not exist if Thou wert not in me? Because I am not yet in hell, though Thou art even there; for if I go down into hell Thou art there. I could not therefore exist, could not exist at all, O my God, unless Thou wert in me. Or should I not rather say, that I could not exist unless I were in Thee from whom are all things, by whom are all things, in whom are all things? Even so, Lord; even so. Where do I call Thee to, since Thou art in me, or whence canst Thou come into me? For where outside heaven and earth can I go that from thence my God may come into me who has said, I fill heaven and earth?

Since, then, Thou fillest heaven and earth, do they contain Thee? Or, as they contain Thee not, dost Thou fill them, and yet there remains something over? And where dost Thou pour forth that which remaineth of Thee when the heaven and earth are filled? Or, indeed, is there no need that Thou who containest all things shouldest be contained of any, since those things which Thou fillest Thou fillest by containing them? For the vessels which Thou fillest do not sustain Thee, since should they even be broken Thou wilt not be poured forth. And when Thou art poured forth on us, Thou are not cast down, but we are uplifted; nor art Thou dissipated, but we are drawn together. But, as Thou fillest all things, dost Thou fill them with Thy whole self, or, as even all things cannot altogether contain Thee, do they contain a part, and do all at once contain the same part? Or has each its own proper part—the greater more, the smaller less? Is, then, one part of Thee greater, another less? Or is it that Thou are wholly everywhere whilst nothing altogether contains Thee?

What, then, art Thou, O my God—what, I ask, but the Lord God? For who is Lord but the Lord? or who is God save our God? Most high, most excellent, most potent, most omnipotent; most merciful and most just; most hidden and most near; most beauteous and most strong, stable, yet contained of none; unchangeable, yet changing all things; never new, never old; making all things new, yet bringing old age upon the proud and they know it not; always working, yet ever at rest; gathering, yet needing nothing; sustaining, pervading and protecting; creating, nourishing, and developing; seeking, and yet possessing all things. Thou lovest, and burnest not; art jealous, yet free from care; repentest, and hast no sorrow; art angry, yet serene; changest Thy ways, leaving unchanged Thy plans; recoverest what Thou findest, having yet never lost; art never in want, whilst Thou rejoicest in gain; never covetous, though requiring usury. That Thou mayest owe, more than enough is given to Thee; yet who hath anything that is not Thine? Thou payest debts while owing nothing; and when Thou forgivest debts, losest nothing. Yet, O my God, my life, my holy joy, what is this that I have said? And what saith any man when he speaks of Thee? Yet woe to them that keep silence, seeing that even they who say most are as the dumb.

> (Saint Augustine, *The Confessions.* Book I Chapters 2, 3, and 4. Quoted from *Basic Writings of Saint Augustine.* Whitney J. Oates, editor (New York: Random House, 1948), Volume I.)

To the above quotations should be added the passage from the *Confessions* Book VII Chapter 10 which I have quoted and discussed at length on pp. 102, 103.

FROM WILLIAM TEMPLE

But the contention that God is the explanation of the world because He is Person or Spirit does mean that if all else but God were abolished, God would still be Himself, whole and entire, capable of creating another world to take the place of the world which had gone out of existence. If God is Personal, He must express Himself; the Word was in the beginning with God; but His self-expression is not the self expressed; that remains always cause, never effect. (p. 265.)

If we adopt this view, we shall have also to hold that no Law of Nature as discovered by physical science is ultimate. It is a general statement of that course of conduct in Nature which is sustained by the purposive action of God so long and so far as it will serve His purpose. No doubt it is true that the same cause will always produce the same effect in the same circumstances. Our contention is that an element in every actual cause, and indeed the determinant element, is the active purpose of God fulfilling itself with that perfect constancy which calls for an infinite graduation of adjustments in the process. Where any adjustment is so considerable as to attract notice it is called miracle; but it is not a specimen of a special class, it is an illustration of the general character of the World-Process. (p. 267.)

This is not a popular doctrine in an age for which the metaphysics of every question is overshadowed by the physics, as in an earlier period the physics was by the metaphysics. Yet I am very sure that the conception of the Divine Personality is only tenable if it is taken in bitter earnest. And then it leads us to the conviction that the immanent principle of the World Process is a purposive Mind, guiding the movement of electrons and of galaxies by the requirements of its unchanging purpose, so that for the most part their course is constant, but the cause of their constancy is itself the cause of their variation when that serves the one purpose best. (p. 269.)

The mistake was to admit the assertion of natural uniformity at the physical level, or to suppose that variations in it must be due to the introduction of some power not normally utilized or the action of some 'higher law' not normally operative. Obviously it has a provisional truth, which has been enough to carry science to its victories. (pp. 287, 288.)

We are left with this result: a purely transcendent God, who intervenes often to give special direction to the course of events, is incompatible with a scientific apprehension of the world; while a purely transcendent

God who never intervenes at all, or has done so only once or twice in recorded history, is incompatible with vital religion. The only way to hold together a vital religion and a scientific apprehension of the world is to assert some form of Divine Immanence.

We do a great disservice alike to philosophy and to religion if we minimize the divergence of the tendencies proper to science and to religion at this point. Because science works with uniformities it is unable to allow in its own processes for any variability in nature; and it is not easy for the men of science to admit that such variability may be real, even though science can take no account of it. Similarly because religion is concerned with Divine Personality it must assert the variability of a natural order which is the expression of that Personality, though for such variation, as for constancy, there must be 'sufficient reason.' (p. 293.)

This position should not involve difficulty for any except believers in mechanical Determinism. If in any sense man has freedom to choose and to act on his choice, this of itself involves a breach in the rigid uniformity of nature. I am free to choose whether I shall stand still or walk across the room. If I choose the latter, I effect a redistribution of the mass of the world and shift its centre of gravity. That I only do so to an extent negligible in the most precise astronomical calculation possible to man, does not affect the principle. And if I can do this to any extent at all, then God, if He exists, can do it to any extent that He pleases. (p. 295.)

So the Personal Deity universally immanent—the Logos—may for centuries act in ways that very imperfectly disclose His Character; yet when time is appropriate may Himself submit to conditions which reveal that Character as it had always been. There is no novelty of causal energy. If He use some way of becoming Himself an historical episode other than that by which other similar episodes are initiated, such for example as birth from a Virgin, this is no manifestation of new and usually dormant power, but is due to the same cause as other and normal births, namely, the Will of this same Logos, now aiming at a special and unique result. In other words, if the immanent principle is personal, we must not only see the whole universe as the expression and utterance of His activity, but must expect to find in its course special characteristic and revealing acts, which are no more truly His than the rest, but do more fully express Him than the rest.

There is ground for believing that there are infinite gradations of such adjustment and adaptation as find their climax in these alleged revelatory acts. The actual practice of religion in any of its forms admits men to experience of the personal action of God in many degrees of self-disclosure. This field has not been worked over by scientific students of the subject with the diligence which it deserves. That is natural enough, because precise and critical observation is very difficult and experiment is from the nature of the case impossible. What is very startling to the philosopher whose mental habit is controlled by scientific interests is the abundance of testimony given by those who have had intimate experience of men's spiritual life to the conviction that in the early stages prayer receives literal fulfillment with great frequency; that later on this becomes less frequent, until it seems almost to cease, as though God at first gives encouragement of the most obvious kind and later withdraws this in order to evoke a deeper trust. Such theories call for scientific investigation; the evidence should be weighed and tested. But if this very common assertion of the persons best qualified to know is well founded, it indicates not only a power, but a readiness, to practise with much freedom that adaptation to circumstances which we have asserted as a necessary inference from the Personality of God. (pp. 296, 297.)

For the most part we shall expect to find, as we find in fact, a widespread uniformity; because where there is no special and sufficient occasion for variation, its occurrence would argue caprice rather than constancy. Moreover, we have seen that, so far as the moral quality of human life is matter of concern to the Creator, it supplies a reason, not so much for variation to meet special contingencies as for a uniformity sufficiently general to be the basis of purposive action. But where there is sufficient occasion, the creative will may vary its more usual activity; when this occurs, it is not through the intrusion of some normally inoperative cause, but through the action of what alone accounts for all existences and occurrences, the volition of personal Deity. It is thus characteristic of God that He should usually act by what to us is uniformity (though the appearance even of this may conceal variations too delicate for our perception and too small to affect our confidence in action), just as it is characteristic of Him to vary His action when the occasion is sufficient. (p. 302.)

(William Temple, *Nature, Man and God* (London: Macmillan and Co., Limited, 1951).)

APPENDIX B

REINHOLD NIEBUHR'S REDEFINITION OF STANDARD CHRISTIAN TERMS (THEOLOGICALLY ARRANGED)

GOD THE CREATOR. "In the Jewish-Christian tradition this problem of pessimism and optimism is solved by faith in a transcendent God who is at once the creator of the world (source of its meaning) and judge of the world (*i.e.,* goal of its perfection)." (CPP. p. 180a.)

CREATION. "We are deceivers yet true, when we say that God created the world. Creation is a mythical idea which cannot be fully rationalized." (BT. p. 7cd.)

DEMONIC. "But it is not free of the demonic pretensions which express themselves whenever a partial human value is given absolute significance by religious emotion." (CPP. p. 192de.)

WRATH OF GOD. "The wrath of God is the world in its essential structure reacting against the sinful corruptions of that structure." ((2)HD. p. 56b.)

MIRACLE. "But we do not believe in the virgin birth, and we have difficulty with the physical resurrection of Christ. We do not believe, in other words, that revelatory events validate themselves by a divine breakthrough in the natural order." (CRPP. p. 198bc.) "The final pinnacle of the Christian faith is this confidence in the completion of life's meaning by the power of God. This pinnacle of faith. . . . has no support from miraculous facts in history." (FH. p. 150ab.)

MYTH. "In one sense all Orthodox Christian theology has

195

been guilty of the sin of profanity. It has insisted on the literal and historic truth of its myths, forgetting that it is the function and character of religious myth to speak of the eternal in relation to time, and that it cannot therefore be a statement of temporal sequences." (CPP. pp. 220f, 221a.)

CHRIST. "The God of our devotion is veritably revealed most adequately in the most perfect personality we know, as he is potentially revealed in all personal values; and his conflict with the inertia of the concrete and historical world is expressed most vividly in the cross of Christ. When dealing with life's ultimates, symbolism is indispensable, and a symbolism which has a basis in historic incident is most effective." (DCNR. p. 237ab.)

INCARNATION. "The significance of Jesus for the religious life of the Western world is due to his attainment and incarnation of a spiritual and moral ideal of such absolute and transcendent nature that none of his followers have been able to compromise it by their practical adjustments to the social necessities of their day." (DCNR. p. 80a-c.)

CHRIST'S RESURRECTION. "Yet honest scholarship must admit that the resurrection is not as well attested as an historical event as the crucifixion." (SDH. p. 237a.) "The idea of the resurrection of the body can of course not be literally true." (BT. p. 290b.) "The self has a unity between this freedom of the spirit and the organism of its body and soul, which makes the emancipation of an immortal soul from a mortal body unthinkable." (SDH. p. 237f.)

CHRIST THE SECOND ADAM. "To say that the innocency of Adam before the fall can be restored only in terms of the perfection of Christ is to assert that life *can approach its original innocency only by aspiring to its unlimited end.*" ((2)HD. p. 77c.)

GRACE. "Essentially the experience of grace in religion is

196

the apprehension of the absolute from the perspective of the relative." (REE. p. 281e.)

"Since perfection is love, the apprehension of perfection is at once the means of seeing one's imperfection and the consoling assurance of grace which makes this realization bearable." (REE. p. 285cd.)

" 'Nature' in this case represents the historical possibilities of justice. 'Grace' would correspond to ideal possibility of perfect love, in which all inner contradictions within the self, and all conflicts and tensions between the self and the other are overcome by the complete obedience of all wills to the will of God." ((2) HD. p. 246bc.)

JUSTIFICATION. "All men who live with any degree of serenity live by some assurance of grace. In every life there must at least be times and seasons when the good is felt as a present possession and not as a far-off goal. The sinner must feel himself 'justified,' that is, he must feel that his imperfections are understood and sympathetically appreciated as well as challenged." (REE. pp. 284f, 285ab.)

OTHER-WORLDLINESS. "If they (men) are to develop a perfect ethical freedom which makes no compromises with life's immediate necessities, they must find a content and a meaning in life beyond its present conflict of interests and desires. That is other-worldliness." (DCNR. p. 242ab.)

KINGDOM OF GOD. "The cross was inspired by a devotion to a 'kingdom which is not of this world'; but the cross was also the method by which that kingdom was changed from an ethereal to a concrete reality. It is the absolute ideal which has no basis in concrete reality which moves men to defy the limitations of the concrete and overcome them." (DCNR. p. 177bc.)

MESSIANIC REIGN. "As [with] most biblical symbols dealing with the eternal fulfillment of the course of history, the 'end of history' in the Messianic reign must not be taken literally. It must nevertheless be taken seriously because it indicates the eternal dimension in which history moves." (DST. p. 96ab.)

CHRIST THE JUDGE OF THE WORLD. ". . . Christ who will be the judge of history. Christ as judge means that when the historical confronts the eternal it is judged by its own ideal possibility, and not by the contrast between the finite and the eternal character of God." ((2)HD. pp. 291e-292a.)

RESURRECTION. "No sign can be given but that of the prophet Jonah, by which Jesus meant the sign of death and resurrection. This is to say, whenever the vicissitudes from which the self, either individually or collectively, suffers are appropriated by faith as divine judgments and not as meaningless caprice, they result in the love, joy, and peace of a new life." (CRPP. p. 203ab.)

"Stoic wisdom is a good antidote to man's whining inclination to deny the fact of his mortality." (FH. p. 63d.)

APPENDIX C

THE INCONSISTENCY BETWEEN REINHOLD NIEBUHR'S RELIGIOUS LONGING AND THE STRUCTURE OF HIS THEOLOGICAL BELIEF

SOME PEOPLE WHO read this book will feel that I have been unfair to Reinhold Niebuhr's thought and have described it as less orthodox than as a matter of fact it is. They will also consider it unfair that I have drawn my evidence from his earlier as well as his later writings. I believe these people are mistaken on both counts.

The factor that has played havoc from the first with the basic interrelated structure of his belief is his inability to describe a relationship between science (which he accepts uncritically) and Biblical religion. As his thought does not progress in this area, the whole constellation of doctrines upon which this problem presses has a basically static quality in his thought. His youthful position is enlarged upon but without progression. As so much of his creative thinking has developed along political, economic, ethical, and social lines it is understandable that even as robustly creative a thinker as Niebuhr should have lacked time to develop progressively all areas of his thinking. Unfortunately the point at which the lack of development comes is the science and religion issue that for the last hundred years has bedeviled theologians, from outstanding writers to local pastors. In order to show that Niebuhr's thought is still deflected from basic Christianity by this problem through his maturity I append here a series of quotations taken exclusively from

Faith and History (first published in 1949) and *The Self and the Dramas of History* (first published in 1955).

But Reinhold Niebuhr is also a Christian who loves the Bible and its teaching. And this love, imbedded in the piety of his personal life, shows through in his writing. His writings contain, therefore, both ideas that he believes, which form the structure of his theological thought (which is sub-Christian), intermingled with Biblical ideas that he yearningly loves but does not believe to be true. I append a selection of these latter expressions quoted exclusively from *Faith and History* and *The Self and the Dramas of History*.

These two types of ideas coexist uneasily in his spirit with an unresolved inconsistency that has about it the naïveté of the integrity of true greatness. There are very few religious writers who permit the reader to watch their thinking in process with all the accompanying bewilderment of life at its growing edge to the extent to which Niebuhr permits it. This is an aspect of the prophetic quality of his writing and it is one reason why his books will continue to be read long after the works of many tidier thinkers are forgotten. But it also makes his theological writings dangerous for a superficial reader of less integrity. For the torrential *mélange* of his writing gives a first impression of much closer approximation to Orthodoxy than the structure of his thought permits. Because of this Niebuhr has unintentionally added to the theological confusion of our time by furnishing generations of theological students with a gold mine of pulpit material which makes their sermons sound like a return to Biblical religion without in fact being so. Thus in preaching they are enabled to avoid the academic embarrassment and integrity of actually subscribing to basic New Testament beliefs and consistently attempting to think through their religious position accordingly. And they are also enabled to avoid the alternative embarrassment and integrity of frankly admitting publicly that the religion they advocate is post-Christian and non-Biblical.

BELIEFS TO WHICH REINHOLD NIEBUHR SUBSCRIBES

"The cultural obscurantism of this kind of literalism not only brings Christian truth in contradiction with the facts, known by natural science and indisputable on their own level. It also makes that truth completely irrelevant to the truths discovered by the social, political, psychological, and historical sciences." (FH. p. 167b.)

"Religious faith in both Catholic and Protestant versions of Christianity and in the Jewish version of Biblical faith survives most vitally in the backward 'regions,' that is, in those sections of culture in which the failure of religion to come to terms with the undoubted truths disclosed by the disciplines of philosophy and the sciences is not found too embarrassing." (SDH. p. 147bc.)

"Thus the encounter of the self with God is defined in

IDEAS REINHOLD NIEBUHR LOVES BUT DOES NOT BELIEVE TO BE TRUE

"This volume is written on the basis of the faith that the Gospel of Christ is true for men of every age and that Jesus Christ is 'the same yesterday, today and forever.' " (FH. p. viie.)

"But the clue to the mystery is the *Agape* of Christ. It is the clue to the mystery of Creation. 'All things were made by him; and without him was not any thing made that was made' (John 1:3)." (FH. p. 233 bc.)

" 'Can any hide himself in secret places that I shall

Biblical faith in terms of a norm which has been set by an historical 'revelation.' And this revelation is an historical event or series of events which are not essentially miraculous (miracles such as the 'virgin birth' are afterthoughts) but are events in history which are discerned by faith to have revelatory power into the ultimate mystery." (SDH. p. 66c.)

". . . certainly invalidates all hopes of heaven which rest upon the idea that an 'immortal 'soul' or mind may escape a mortal body." (SDH. p. 242b.)

". . . which makes the emancipation of an immortal soul from a mortal body unthinkable." (SDH. p. 237f.)

"Honest scholarship must admit that the resurrection is not as well attested as an historical event as the crucifixion." (SDH. p. 237a.)

"But the final proof of man's creaturely limit is a fact in his individual life: his death. The same man who creates and recreates historic institutions, who seeks to understand nature

not see him? saith the Lord,' Jeremiah continues, 'Do not I fill heaven and earth? saith the Lord. I have heard what the prophets said, that prophesy lies in my name, saying, I have dreamed. . . . The prophet that hath a dream, let him tell a dream; and he that hath my word, let him speak my word faithfully.' (Jeremiah 23: 24 - 28)" (SDH. p. 86de.)

"The relation of the Son to the Father is most simply stated in the Scriptural word: 'God so loved the world, that he gave his only begotten Son, that whosoever believeth in him should not perish, but have eternal life' (John 3:16)." (FH. p. 168a.)

". . . in the life, death and resurrection of Christ we have the key to the mercy and love of God . . ." (SDH p.224f.)

"In Christian thought the

and history, who holds past events in memory and future events in prospect, dies just as those animals die who have no commerce with any of these wider structures of meaning." (FH. p. 77cd.)

" '. . . do not complain because it will perish after it has consumed thee,' declares Aurelius. The advice may be regarded as a wholesome reminder of human creatureliness. Indeed Stoic wisdom is a good antidote to man's whining inclination to deny the fact of his mortality." (FH. p. 63d.)

"Such a faith may easily degenerate into an hysterical claim to the 'right' of immortality, in which case it becomes a transcendental version of the old sin of trying too desperately to live." (FH. p. 176c.)

"There is the question of whether the experience of the 'living Lord' was not the private experience of his disciples and was later justified and made more vivid by the story of the empty tomb." (SDH. p. 237b.)

resurrection of Christ is, however, not only indicative of the triumph of Christ over sin in the very Cross which seemed to make him its victim, but also is proof of God's power to overcome death. St. Paul, in fact, deduces both the resurrection from the dead and the triumph over sin from Christ's resurrection." (FH. p. 149 cd.)

". . . to see, in other words, the whole mystery of God's mercy disclosed is to know that the crucified Lord had triumphed over death and 'when he had by himself purged our sins, sat down on the right hand of the Majesty on high' (Hebrews 1 :3)." (FH. pp. 147de, 148a.)

"Thus the church has the sacrament of baptism in which 'we are buried with him by baptism into death: that like as Christ was raised from the dead by the glory of the Father, even so we should also walk in newness of life' (Romans 6:4)." (FH. p. 240ef.)

"The creed ends with three affirmations in a significant order: 'I believe in . . . the forgiveness of sins: the resurrection of the body: and the life everlasting.' " (SDH. p. 238c.)

"The hope that both the individual and the total drama of life will end in 'the forgiveness of sins: the resurrection of the body: and the life everlasting'. . ." (SDH. p. 240f.)

"While the self is a unique center of life it is indeterminately 'open' to other selves. There are no geographic or temporal limits for the self's dialogue with others. Some of the significant dialogues are carried on with heroes of the past or with a deceased parent or absent lover. The dialogue in such cases may seem to lack the 'other,' so necessary for the dialogue. But memories will furnish the stuff for the dialogue which are almost as powerful as contemporary exchanges." (SDH. p. 33bc.)

"For all the therapeutic skill of Freudian psychology, and its wisdom in exploring the labyrinths of the self, it has confused the realities of the internal dialogue in some degree by obscuring the fact that the self is really in both the 'id' and the 'super-ego.' " (SDH. p. 9bc.)

"These eschatological expectations in New Testament faith, however embarrassing when taken literally, are necessary for a Christian interpretation of history." (FH. p. 214d.)

"If, then, it is impossible to define the end of history as a particular event in history and since the end as *Telos* lies outside of history, the question arises why the Biblical symbols should be taken seriously at all." (FH. p. 237c.)

"On these grounds the Christ event was recognized to be the 'end' of history, not in the sense of its 'finis' but as its *telos*. History would go on, and human pride and arrogance would create unimaginable evils. But nothing would surprise or dismay the person who had once penetrated to the mystery by the help of this key." (SDH. p. 91ef.)

"The modern experience. . . . It is therefore incapable either of rising to a tragic defiance of destiny, as de-

"The supreme sacrament of the Christian church, the Lord's Supper, is filled with this eschatological tension. It is instituted with the words: 'This do in remembrance of me.' St. Paul declares that 'as often as ye eat this bread, and drink this cup, ye do shew the Lord's death *till he come.*' (I Corinthians 11:26). Thus in this Sacrament the Christian community lives by a great memory and a great hope." (FH. p. 241 ab.)

". . .a 'general' resurrection which completes the whole human story, and which is associated with the 'coming again' of the suffering Savior in triumph 'with great power and glory.' " (SDH. p. 238de.)

". . . mankind will continue to 'see through a glass darkly' and the final meaning can be anticipated only by faith. It awaits a completion when 'we shall know even as we are known.' " (FH. p. 214b.)

picted in Greek drama, or of achieving a renewal of life through a contrite submission to destiny, as in Christian tragedy." (FH. p. 9ab.)

"Nations, as well as individuals, may be destroyed not only by violating the laws of life, but also by achieving a defenceless purity, incompatible with the necessities of survival. Ultimately New Testament faith was to revere a Christ whose perfect goodness was validated by an obvious defeat in history." (FH. p. 128b.)

"The Christ was expected to be a triumphant Messiah, and he is in fact a 'suffering servant' who does not bring the struggle between good and evil to a triumphant conclusion." (SDH. p. 91cd.)

"The ultimate question always remains whether the mystery is so absolute as to annul the meaning of the historical drama or whether there is a key of meaning in the mystery, a 'light that shineth in darkness,' which clarifies, rather than annuls, all the strange and variegated dramas of human history." (SDH. p. 242f.)

"The Christian awaits a 'general resurrection' as well as a 'last judgment.' " (FH. p. 214cd.)

" 'Fear not them,' declares Christ, 'which kill the body, but are not able to kill the soul: but rather fear him which is able to destroy both soul and body in hell' (Matthew 10:28)." (FH. pp. 175f,176a.)

"According to the New Testament. . . . They will not be surprised or dismayed by anything, knowing 'that neither life nor death . . . will separate them from the love of God which is in Christ Jesus our Lord.' " (FH. p. 28de.)

BIBLIOGRAPHY

To simplify the references to Niebuhr's works I have mentioned them in the footnotes by initials only. A reference's location on the page is indicated by the letters a b c d e f. The location is obtained by laying a six inch ruler along the margin of the page. The first inch of printing is "a." The sixth inch of printing is "f," etc.

BT	Niebuhr, Reinhold, *Beyond Tragedy* (New York: Charles Scribner's Sons, 1955).
CLCD	*The Children of Light and the Children of Darkness* (New York: Charles Scribner's Sons, 1953).
CPP	*Christianity and Power Politics* (New York: Charles Scribner's Sons, 1948).
CRPP	*Christian Realism and Political Problems* (New York: Charles Scribner's Sons, 1953).
DCNR	*Does Civilization Need Religion?* (New York: The Macmillan Company, 1929).
DST	*Discerning the Signs of the Times* (New York: Charles Scribner's Sons, 1946).
EAC	*Essays in Applied Christianity* (New York: Meridian Books, 1959).
FH	*Faith and History* (New York: Charles Scribner's Sons, 1951).
(2)HD	*The Nature and Destiny of Man, Vol. II Human Destiny* (New York: Charles Scribner's Sons, 1943).
(1)HN	*The Nature and Destiny of Man, Vol. I Human Nature* (New York: Charles Scribner's Sons, 1941).
IAH	*The Irony of American History* (New York: Charles Scribner's Sons, 1954).
ICE	*An Interpretation of Christian Ethics* (New York: Harper & Brothers, 1935).
LNTC	*Leaves from the Notebook of a Tamed Cynic* (New York: Willett, Clark & Colby, 1929).
MMIS	*Moral Man and Immoral Society* (New York: Charles Scribner's Sons, 1955).

PSA   *Pious and Secular America* (New York: Charles
             Scribner's Sons, 1958).
REE   *Reflections on the End of an Era* (New York: Charles
             Scribner's Sons, 1934).
SDH   *The Self and the Dramas of History* (New York:
             Charles Scribner's Sons, 1955).
SNE   *The Structure of Nations and Empires* (New York:
             Charles Scribner's Sons, 1959).
T in M   "The Truth in Myths," in Bixler, J.S., editor, *The
             Nature of Religious Experience Essays in Honor of
             Douglas Clyde Macintosh* (New York: Harper and
             Brothers, 1937).

Augustine, Saint, *Basic Writings of Saint Augustine* Oates, Whitney
    J., editor (New York: Random House, 1948), Vol. I. *The
    Confessions.*
Baillie, John, *The Idea of Revelation in Recent Thought* (New
    York: Columbia University Press, 1956).
Carnell, Edward J., *The Theology of Reinhold Niebuhr* (Grand
    Rapids, Mich.: Wm. B. Eerdman's Publishing Company, 1951).
Davidman, Joy, *Smoke on the Mountain* (Philadelphia: The West-
    minster Press, 1954).
Gunther, John, *Inside U.S.A.* (New York: Harper and Brothers,
    1947).
Harland, Gordon, *The Thought of Reinhold Niebuhr* (New York:
    Oxford University Press, 1960).
Hofmann, Hans, *The Theology of Reinhold Niebuhr* (New York:
    Charles Scribner's Sons, 1956).
Hutcheson, Harold R., editor and translator, *Lord Herbert of Cher-
    bury's De Religione Laici . . . with a Critical Discussion of his
    Life and Philosophy* (New Haven: Yale University Press, 1944).
Kegley, Charles W. and Bretall, Robert W., editors, *Reinhold Nie-
    buhr His Religious, Social, and Political Thought* (New York:
    The Macmillan Company, 1956).
King, Rachel H., *George Fox and the Light Within, 1650-1660*
    (Philadelphia: Friends Book Store, 1940).
————, *Theology You can Understand* (New York: Morehouse-
    Gorham Co., 1956).
Knight, William Allen, *The Song of Our Syrian Guest* (New York:
    The Pilgrim Press, 1906).

Phillips, J. B., *Letters to Young Churches* (New York: The Macmillan Company, 1957).

Pollard, William G., *Chance and Providence God's Action in a World Governed by Scientific Law* (New York: Charles Scribner's Sons, 1958).

Revised Standard Version of the Holy Bible (New York: Thomas Nelson and Sons, 1952).

Schrödinger, Erwin, *Mind and Matter* (Cambridge: At the University Press, 1958).

Soper, David Wesley, *Major Voices in American Theology* (Philadelphia: The Westminster Press, 1953).

Temple, William, *Nature, Man and God* (London: Macmillan and Co., 1951).

Underhill, Evelyn, *Mysticism a Study in the Nature and Development of Man's Spiritual Consciousness* (New York: E. P. Dutton and Company, 1911).

Whale, J.S., *Christian Doctrine* (New York: The Macmillan Company, 1941).